'What did you do in the War, Grandma?'

Doreen Wildgoose

Sheaf Publishing • Sheffield

First published in 1995 by Sheaf Publishing Ltd,
35 Mooroaks Road, Sheffield 10

ISBN: 185048 015 X

*In August 1939 at Cleethorpes, from left to
right are Doreen, Margaret and Hilda.
The child in front was just passing.*

Contents

For my Grand-daughter,
Rebecca McManus

The day War broke out . . .

I WAS EIGHT YEARS OLD when THE WAR started in 1939. During the run-up I always thought of the War in capital letters, because of the way that grown-ups always referred to it. 'When THE WAR starts', or 'If THE WAR starts', or 'After what he's done to Czechoslovakia, THE WAR is bound to come eventually'. He, of course, being Adolf Hitler.

Hitler was a man who was the source of much merriment amongst the children of my generation. A funny, Chaplinesque little man, with a daft moustache and hair which fell over one eye, we spent many hours in that summer of 1939, singing cheeky songs about all his shortcomings and doing the goose-step up and down the school yard, and generally making a mockery of everything for which he stood. As children, of course, we had no idea what he *really* stood for, but as the next few years passed we soon became aware of it.

We were just an ordinary working-class family, living in an ordinary terraced home with an outside toilet in the backyard and a very small garden, in Ulverston Road. The house is still there and looks much the same from the front as it did then, apart from the much smarter front door, and the new modern windows. There were five of us living there in 1939, Dad and Mum and three daughters; Margaret who was twelve, myself – four years younger – and Hilda, the youngest, who was seven.

On that fateful Sunday in September I wasn't at home when Neville Chamberlain made his broadcast from the Cabinet Room in Downing Street. I was in fact making the short tram journey with my sister, Hilda, to visit Aunty Emily who lived at Heeley. Aunty Emily was aware that the War had been declared, and as I recall she was a little taken aback to see her two small nieces on her doorstep, but there was nothing much that she could do about it, except usher us quickly inside, in case the Germans were following us up the street! To make matters worse, during our short visit the air raid sirens wailed. We had heard them before, of course. Over the past few months we had been treated to many practice runs in case the War broke out, so that everyone would recognise the sound and take shelter. But Aunty Emily didn't have a shelter. I think it was because before this sunny September day, she hadn't expected a war to break out overnight, but I'm afraid she hadn't reckoned on the Germans marching into Poland at the crack of dawn.

However, in the event she knew exactly what to do. Together with cousin Jean, she sat us on the stairs with a cupful of water each. I have never been quite sure whether the water was meant for drinking or whether it was intended for use in dealing with any stray incendiary bomb which may be dropped on the neighbourhood. In either case, I remember that I drank mine. Sitting on the stairs in the middle of a war is very thirsty work. Besides, I was scared, for I had a good idea what bombs could do.

Sometime during 1936, I was borrowed by Aunty Alice to take part in a demonstration against the Spanish Civil War. I remembered vividly passing Endcliffe Park, lying with other children on the back of a lorry, with bandages covered with red paint wrapped around most of my extremities. Of course, these bandages were over my winter clothes because, as I recall it was a very cold day, and no doubt Aunty Alice had been forcibly reminded by Mum that she hadn't got the money for Doctor's bills.

The 'All Clear' sounded soon afterwards and we learned later that it had been merely another practice run. We were sent on our way with the strictest of instructions not to call at Grandma's, who was next on our visiting lists, but to go straight home. Being fairly well-behaved children we did exactly that, and arrived home to find Mum and Dad, assisted by Aunty Alice from next door, putting up blackout curtains to all the windows.

So, on that beautiful September day when Adolf Hitler ignored the ultimatum to withdraw his troops from Poland, my sisters and I began

2

to learn that the German leader was no longer a figure of fun, but rather that he was the person who would be responsible for turning our lives upside down during the rest of our childhood, and for bringing great hardship and misery to almost every family in the country.

As the days went by, a new word, which was to stay with us until well into my marriage in 1951, crept into everyone's vocabulary – rationing. Although we hadn't lived exactly like royalty during the first years of the 'Hungry Thirties', at least we had been used to adequate plain food, and I cannot remember ever being hungry as a child. But this, I am sure, owed more to Mum's management skills than anything else, especially during Dad's illness in 1937, when a serious heart condition kept him off work for almost the whole of the year (and which incidently kept him out of the armed forces throughout the war), but rationing? That was an entirely different thing.

Thursday was our rations day and it quickly became the most important day of the week. It was quite exciting really, one never knew if some shipment or other of tinned fruit, or salmon or anything at all out of the ordinary had arrived. If so, one could come home with one tin per family or maybe two ounces per person of something special. It didn't happen very often, though, and to see Mum juggling with the basic rations for five was a sight to behold. Round about Tuesday we would all peer gloomily into the sugar basin and the few spoonfuls left in it, knowing full well that no more sugar, in it's bright blue packet, would be available until Thursday, when Mum went to the Co-op.

Basic rations meant exactly that, *basic*. Each member of each family was issued with a ration book and was entitled to a fixed amount of any food which was in short supply, each week. Butter,lard, sugar, bacon, eggs, tea and meat were all rationed in this way, and although the exact amounts allowed varied as the War continued, I'm fairly sure it was mainly in the area of two ounces per ration book. We were allowed one egg a week, as well, unless the hens were laying particularly well, in which case we were allowed two, and could maybe have an omelette. And that was per person, weekly.

Normally, eggs were only used in cooking, and this early in the war, that great American export and life-saver of every British housewife, the dried egg, had not yet made its historic appearance. Many other goods were considered to be luxuries, dried fruit, for example and most things in tins and jars, including preserves, and these were doled out under a points system. These points were printed in the backs of all ration books, and were cut out by the retailer in exchange for goods of the holder's choice, depending on availability, which probably accounted for the fact that we usually had adequate jam, but very little in the way of pineapple chunks.

Bread was rationed later on in the war but it was always fairly plentiful, even if it was a funny off-white colour. There was always a lot of joking about the bread. Whatever happened, flu, measles, pregnancies, some wag would trot out the line, 'I blame the bread'. Funny the things that make one laugh in wartime.

For our meat ration we were registered with Dewhursts, at the bottom of Woodseats Road, and shopping there was an adventure in itself. It really all depended on what was available at the time of purchase, and often part of the weekly ration had to be taken in corned beef, much to Mum's chagrin. Offal was a prize much sought-after, and steak became almost a dream – although in our house it always had been – but we managed, and funnily enough we never seemed to ail much, despite the shortages. It must have been a healthy diet, come to think of it; we seemed to eat mountains of vegetables, so today's vegetarians have probably got it right.

Dad's cigarettes were always a problem purchase, but the bush telegraph in our neighbourhood worked pretty well. Washing was left in the

tub, and windows were left half-cleaned when the word went out that 'Cigs had arrived at the Co-op', or in some cases Shentalls, which was a large grocery shop on Abbeydale Road facing the Co-op, depending on where one was registered for rations. If we were unlucky enough to be on holiday from school when the call came, we had to go and queue all round the shop to 'save Mum a job', as she would say. I don't know what happened to the law which forbade selling cigarettes to children under sixteen, it never seemed to apply to us. Maybe it was because they were in such short supply, and there was such a high demand that we would never have dared to a face fag-less, short-tempered Dad if we went home without them.

We got used to eating many peculiar things, which ingenious people concocted during the war years. Jam was always a good thing to have on the pantry, especially when there were three children in the house with the usual childish appetites, and jam was not rationed, or 'off-ration' as we used to call it. It was a house rule that precious butter and margarine were not used under anything which could be spread on a slice of bread, so consequently jam, golden syrup and lemon curd would soak through the bread and be almost unpalatable Once, Mum, who had never made jam before (and as far as I knew, never did so again) found, from somewhere, a recipe for rhubarb and date jam. No matter what she did with it and how many times she boiled it up again, that jam was never going to set, but we all had to eat it .

Nothing was ever wasted, so we ploughed through about twelve jars of the stuff. It wouldn't spread, of course, so we just did the best we could, as it ran down the knife and soaked immediately through the bread. 'Plenty of children in Europe would be glad of that', Mum used to say, and she was right, of course, but we didn't appreciate the senti-ment, and thought dark thoughts like 'they can have it, and welcome'.

Mum would do strange things with the butter and marg ration, too. I think she put it all together and added milk, I'm not sure of the details, but it finished up in one hard, unspreadable mess in a basin. Dad called it 'a mess of potage'.

A friend of mine once told me that her father grew hundreds of turnips on his allotment and, to save them rotting in the ground, he strung them up all round the attic. They ate them for months. I don't know what they tasted like in the end, but she looked well enough.

Margaret – my elder sister – was four years older than me, and one day when Mum was out she decided to bake a tray of lemon tarts. We all set to with a will, but when they came out of the oven, they were not fit to eat. Fearing reprisals when Mum returned, we threw them in the bin. We didn't have the savvy to hide them under the ashes, and of course, Mum discovered them. She went spare, and after hidings all round she threatened us with Lord Woolton. Lord Woolton was the Food Minister at the time, and although I knew little about politics I know that it was an offence to waste food and I knew that Lords wore ermine capes and coronets.

For days afterwards I was on the look-out for anyone fitting this description, coming to the house to take us all three to prison. Nobody came, of course, but we never tried to 'save Mum a job' again.

Getting used to making do . . .

WINTERTIME is never the best time for children to get rid of their surplus energy, except when the snows come and sledges can be brought out from their summer hibernation, but that first winter of the war provided us with many hours of exciting things to do. Soldiers were billeted in the grounds of Abbeydale Grange school, and one morning a sentry box appeared at the bottom of the drive in Bannerdale Road. After giving much thought to this happening and discussing it at great length in the school yard at Carterknowle, we decided that, where there is a sentry box, there are soldiers changing guard. I think someone had seen it in London, a place not too familiar to most of us.

So, each day the soldiers were treated, whenever we were out of school, to groups of children standing around the gate, waiting expectantly for the relief guard, accompanied by the fire-breathing sergeant, to march down the drive. There was always lots of shouting and stamping of heavily-booted feet, and strangely enough they didn't seem to mind us doing exactly the same thing about six yards away. Occasionally the sergeant, depending on his mood, would tell us to 'Gerrout of it', but the interest had palled by the time the guard had changed, anyhow, so we went merrily on our way, either to school or home again, marching in some kind of formation, like the soldiers did.

Once or twice a day during that winter when we were at home we would hear marching feet, and would rush out of the house and down the passage to watch the soldiers, sparks coming from their boot heels in the gloom, marching with their rifles and backpacks, down the road and off into the distance. Some kid or other would make the joke, which we never tired of, 'They're all out of step, but our Joe'. And some

7

woman would probably say, 'I wonder where most of them lads will finish up'. This usually from the lady in the next yard down from us, who had four sons already in the Services.

The Balloon Barrage locations were also very popular that winter. These barrage balloons, filled with hydrogen gas, were a familiar sight during the war. There were hundreds of them dotted about the skies, in every major city and over important target areas, and they were used as a deterrent against enemy planes. Contact with the mooring cable was almost certain to damage the plane or even to bring it down, and I suppose it also prevented the enemy from using low-flying attacks on targets such as munitions factories and railway lines etc. One of my friends earnestly assured me that her dad had told her that the Germans would never get to Sheffield because our balloons were the best in the world. I remember deriving great comfort from her words, even though when I imparted the good news to Mum, she dismissed it as stuff and nonsense, and told me that Enid's dad never did have a deal of sense. Nevertheless, we found these balloons very interesting, and we would go to all the sites, usually in the parks, hoping to see the large, silvery, elephant lookalike balloons, either going up or coming down, which they did at intervals through the day. Sometimes we were lucky, but most times we had just missed it, and would stand around feeling very cheated whilst the object of our interest, just floated about in the sky doing absolutely nothing.

There was also an Auxiliary Fire Station at the end of Archer Road, and after we had gone through the changing of the guard routine, we would cross the almost traffic-free Abbeydale Road (family cars were fairly thin on the ground in our neighbourhood – in fact they were non-existent – there were a few about, but most of these were up on bricks in garages for the duration) and watch the AFS (Auxiliary Fire Service) men going through their routine. This was always a delight to behold. They were all raw recruits to a man, and at this stage in the War they hadn't quite reached the high standard for which they later received the much-deserved credit and heartfelt thanks of the populace, and we spent quite a few happy hours observing them on the forecourt.

Their routine seemed mainly to consist of running around, dragging very cumbersome lengths of hosepipe and trying very hard not to trip each other up, whilst all the while being shouted at by the officer in charge. It has to be remembered that the only fire that most of these men had seen was the one in their grate at home, and they worked hard and mostly cheerfully despite the ribald laughter of a small, but swiftly growing bunch of horrible kids.

All in all, the first winter of the War, referred to afterwards as the phoney war, was not a bad time for children in our area. There was little danger from the air, that came later, and we were getting used to making do – the early thirties had given us a good grounding for that – so we were happy enough. There was also a strong rumour flying round the school yard that soap was going to be rationed, so we thought that in some ways things were actually improving.

In April and May 1940, the War began to take on a different meaning. The Germans invaded Norway and Denmark and then the Low Countries. They then proceeded across Belgium and France and by the end of May had entrapped the British Expeditionary Force within a tiny perimeter in a little-known town on the French coast called Dunkirk. By this time we had a co-alition government, for Winston Churchill had taken over as Prime Minister on May 10th. That news was received with mixed feelings at home, because although Mum had always thought that Chamberlain was useless, well, Churchill was a Tory too, but she said, 'We'll see'.

I only ever remember seeing my mother cry twice. The first was when Edward the Eighth abdicated and sailed away with Wallis Simpson in December 1936, and the second time was when the news came through about Dunkirk. Most families at that time knew someone who had sons, brothers, husbands or fathers who were taken off the beaches at Dunkirk. Hundreds of boats, pleasure craft and small motor launches plied back and forth between the beaches and the ships of the Royal Navy, carrying the exhausted men of the BEF – the British Expeditionary Force, which had gone to France early in the War. In all, they helped to rescue over 330,000 troops in nine days up to June 4th and bring them back to Britain. The civilian boat owners and the men of the Royal Navy shared, with the soldiers of the BEF, the constant bombing and shelling of the Dunkirk beaches, and there were many stories – still told today – of the courage and heroism during the time of 'The Miracle of Dunkirk'.

A few days later, German troops entered Paris, and on 22nd June 1940 an armistice was signed and France surrendered. Mr Churchill told us that 'The Battle of France is over – the Battle of Britain is about to begin'. Stirring stuff, indeed. We stood alone, the only power to remain unconquered who had taken up arms against Hitler in 1939.

The grown-ups around us now expected a very hard time of it, and from the bits of conversation which I understood, one thing was starkly clear. If the Germans came, the first thing to happen in our family would be the incarceration of Aunty Alice and Uncle Ted in something called a Concentration Camp. This fact was absolutely certain, I overheard her tell my mother, because she was a member, together with Uncle Ted, of the Communist Party.

I loved Aunty Alice dearly. My mother was always very busy, catering for the needs of Dad and three growing girls, and it was Aunty Alice next door, who, being childless herself always had time for us. She taught me how to knit and how to enjoy books, and would answer all my questions, which were numerous, having what one of my teachers referred to as an 'inquiring mind', and my mother 'an unhealthy liking of books'.

I had heard of these camps, because a friend of Aunty Alice had living with her family a young Jewish girl – Vera – the daughter of a Prague jeweller. I played with Vera sometimes, and she missed her family very much. She came to England in 1937 from Czechoslovakia, and she had no idea what had happened to her mother and father, but she knew that there were such places in Eastern Europe, and after playing with her for a time, so did I. But neither of us understood what they were all about until a few years afterwards, me from the Newsreel pictures at the end of the War, and Vera when she tried to find her family, and all had perished.

The thought of Aunty Alice and Uncle Ted being taken away to any destination filled me with dread. I prayed fervently, every night for months, that the Germans would not cross the Channel; I wasn't quite sure where the Channel was at that time, but I knew that Hitler had now got easy access to it and could invade at any time.

In the event, the Germans decided to conquer us in the air. On August 13th the Luftwaffe launched its air offensive against Britain. The Battle of Britain truly had begun. The RAF fighter pilots were constantly in the skies over Britain, challenging the German planes which came over in droves to bomb London and other major cities across the country. Fighter Command's achievements are legendary. As well as British pilots, there were Squadrons of Poles, Czechs, Canadians and others who fought the Battle of Britain so heroically that summer and autumn. We didn't see much action as far north as Sheffield. The dogfights between the British fighters and the enemy raiders were mainly over the south coast and southern counties, but there were reports on the radio and in the newsreels at the cinemas. I don't think that we were given all the facts of the desperate situation we were in, and I particularly remember the ultra-cheerful tone and Gung-ho attitude of the newsreel commentators at the time.

London took the brunt of the bombing that autumn, and into the winter, but eventually all the major cities had their share, Coventry, Glasgow, Liverpool – the list was endless – and on the night of December 12th it was the turn of Sheffield. On that Thursday night, and again the following Sunday, we very nearly had the living daylights knocked out of us.

My dad, below, with his three daughters in 1934. I'm in the middle. The photograph was taken behind Grandma's house in Heeley.

The photograph of my Mum and Dad at Cleethorpes was taken in August 1939, and is the only holiday I remember. Holidays were not encouraged during the War.

The Sheffield Blitz

B Y THE AUTUMN OF 1940, most families had some sort of air raid protection, the most popular being the Anderson shelter. These were constructed in back gardens from prefabricated corrugated iron pieces, delivered to the home, and paid for by the Government. There was also the Morrison shelter, which was a re-inforced table-like construction, which became a permanent fixture in the living room until the end of the war, and was used as a table by the family. I only ever saw one of these shelters, when I went on a visit to see Uncle Bill in Portsmouth. This was in 1946, well after the war had ended, and it still had pride of place in the living room (and a very small living room it was) because they were still waiting patiently for the authorities to remove it.

Mum didn't hold with either of these ideas, so after consulting with the neighbours, they decided on the third option, a re-inforced cellar. We lived in the top house of our backyard, and after a visit by the authorities it was decided to re-inforce Mrs Lindsey's cellar. Mrs Lindsey lived in the bottom house. The idea was to make access doors in each cellar, from our house to Mrs Lindsey's, and from her house to two doors below in the next yard. This meant that six families shared one shelter, and it worked very well. At least we had company. There were holes, just big enough to climb through, with proper doors on them, situated about two feet up the wall in each cellar. The one under the passage between Aunty Alice's and Mrs Smith's often posed a bit of a problem for Mum. It was a hands and knees job, and as Mum was no lightweight, and she never went into the shelter without the bag containing the policies under one arm and the bird-cage, complete with budgie in the other hand, it was not really surprising.

These doors never had any locks on them and no-one ever gave it a second thought, but of course that was in the days when one could go out and leave any door unlocked. Recently, when on holiday in the North-east, I overheard a conversation between some elderly day-trippers from Newcastle, and they were chatting about the days when anyone could leave their houses without locking the doors, and one old gentleman said, 'After all, who'd want to pinch an old tabbed rug and a mangle?' My sentiments entirely. In those days, not many people had anything worth stealing, anyhow.

We didn't use the bunk beds very much. These were provided in the shelter, mainly for the children, but it meant carrying the bedding in every time we needed it, because it couldn't be left down there as it was far too damp. When the War was in it's infancy, and we were expecting the worst, Mum did have us sleeping in the shelter, just in case, but we soon got fed up with it after the novelty had worn off, and we were glad to get back to our own beds.

In the beginning, when the siren went, we would climb out of our beds in the middle of the night and flock down to the shelter, but after a while we would just get up and sit in the living room until the all-clear went, and listen if there were any bombs dropping, or any guns firing. Often, the enemy planes were on their way back home after dropping their loads on some other city, and we could just hear the Ack-ack guns trying to shoot them down. It was amazing how blasé we became, and how, just by listening to the Dorniers and Junkers above, even the youngest amongst us could tell by the noise whether they were loaded with bombs or not.

Thursday the 12th December 1940 began just like any other day. It was cold, a typical pre-Christmas day, with excitement in the air at the prospect looming of the school holidays. We didn't expect much for Christmas, because there wasn't much to be had, and anyway, Dad had told us the previous Christmas that Father Christmas had been called up, and was now in the Swiss Navy. (I didn't appreciate that joke until I was much older.) From my lofty, nearly nine-years-old position, I knew that he was only having us on, but I think it helped Hilda, who was younger than I, over the transition period.

Dad went to work as usual. In those days, Mum was often heard to remark that the only bit of walking Dad ever did was down the passage and, depending on the time of day, either turn left to Laycock Engineering or, if it was in the evening, turn right to the Smithywood Working Men's Club. She was right, too, he never wandered far in those days.

At lunchtime, we were all home for dinner – as the mid-day meal was always referred to at home – and if Aunty Alice was home, she would pop in to see us. The 12th was such an ordinary day, I don't think anyone would remember much about it, but after seven in the evening, anyone who was around at the time would probably remember all the details.

We were all in the house after tea that evening, except Dad, who, like many of the men at that time, was working overtime, and expected home about seven-thirty. Whilst we were having tea, Mum had some dough rising in the hearth, ready to get the bread in the oven before Dad got home. When the tea things were cleared away, she kneaded the dough, put it in the tins, and placed them in the oven. As she closed the oven door the siren wailed. We didn't have to wait long before we heard the bombs, they were dropping within minutes, and we were very soon scuttling down the cellar steps, Mum carrying the policies, which were always to hand, and the budgie cage, and bewailing all the while the probable loss of her precious bread. It was just after 7pm.

Most members of the six families were in the shelter that night. Those that weren't were either at work, like Dad, or outside in the thick of it doing a bit of fire-watching. The attack came in three waves, with Junkers, Heinkels and Dornier bombers dropping their loads all across the city. According to figures published later, in all there were approximately 450 high-explosive bombs, six parachute mines (one of them landing on Aunty Nellie's house at Norton) and thousands of incendiary bombs which, according to my husband, were dropped first to light up the City. (Two of these bombs landed, at separate times during the raid, on his mother's roof in Broadfield Road. She told me many years later that she had to cook the Christmas dinner in 1940 with the umbrella up, because one of the holes in the roof was bang over the cooker, and it was raining). The raiders then proceeded up one side of The Moor and down the other, almost destroying the whole of the City Centre.

After the first wave, the bombing eased up a little, and Margaret, my elder sister, volunteered, or rather was volunteered by Mum, to go up and remove the bread from the oven. She returned safely to the shelter and the bread was saved.

As the bombing resumed it seemed to intensify, and Uncle Ted came in to report that bombs were dropping round Laycock's factory just up the road. There was what was termed a bomber's moon that night, and following the railway lines, which were not difficult to see in the bright moonlight, the raiders were dropping their bombs around the factory.

During the first half-hour of the attack, I was expecting Dad to make his way home somehow. After all, it was only a little way away and when he didn't arrive, Mum said that he would be in the air raid shelter at work. We could hear the explosions quite clearly, they seemed to be over the top of us, and it was the most harrowing and frightening experience of my life. The added fear of maybe never seeing Dad alive again made me almost hysterical. Looking back, I don't suppose that I helped much, in a shelter full of people who must have been as scared as I was, but when one is only nine years old, knowing what the night could bring before daylight came, maybe it was understandable. I remember well, Aunty Alice tearing a strip off poor old Uncle Ted, and telling him that he should have more sense than to come into the shelter blurting things like that in front of the children, and him going back outside, suitably chastened, into the thick of it. As it happened, the raiders did little damage to Laycock's factory. Most of the bombs had fallen in the surrounding area, and a lot of damage was done to the houses on Cawthorne Grove, which was just opposite.

Sometime during that terrible night, Mrs Lindsey's daughter, Margaret, came in. She was almost incoherent and nearly unrecognisable. When she was calmer she said that she had made her way home, from Firth Brown's on Carlisle Street where she worked, through the worst of the bombing, to get home. She told her horrified audience that she had dodged from shelter to shelter, through the City centre, and tried to explain the carnage she had seen. Then she said that she had stepped over dummies, blown out of all the shop windows, and I caught some of the grown-ups mouthing silently to each other, 'They'll be bodies, not dummies,' but they wouldn't say it to her face, because she was far too upset.

There were six children in our shelter that night, we three, two from the Pashley family from the top house in the yard below, and baby Rodgerson, who was just a few weeks old, and who slept peacefully through the whole night in a drawer from his mother's dressing table.

Eventually, the All-clear sounded, and that dreadful night was over. We made our way back to our homes, and our beds. Dad came in, almost with the final notes of the siren, none the worse for his night spent in the shelter at work, and at least for our family, all was right with the world again. We had no damage, nor had any of our neighbours, not even a pane of glass was missing from any of our houses. We had been far luckier than most other districts, the only thing that was noticeable at all was the heavy smell of smoke and burning timber and the thick hoar frost which had whitewashed the gardens and the field at the back. It was just after five in the morning.

We awoke later to find what can only be described as an avalanche of refugees. First to arrive were Aunty Nelly and Uncle Henry, Dad's sister and her husband, who had lost everything when one of the six landmines to drop on Sheffield had landed on their home at Norton. About an hour later, it was the turn of Aunty Alice and Uncle Ted to receive unexpected visitors, when Uncle's mother, brother Albert (who was on leave from the army) and his wife arrived. They all three lived together in Annesley Road at Greenhill, and had been temporarily evacuated from their area because of an unexploded bomb which had landed in a neighbour's garden.

A little while after them came Aunty Emily, Uncle Charlie and Jean, accompanied by Uncle Charlie's brother, who was a Naval Officer also on leave, his wife and small child. Ironically they had arrived in Sheffield the day before on a short visit from Portsmouth, mainly to get away from the bombing for a while. And last but not least, came Grandpa Wilson. Grandma and Grandpa lived within 200 yards of Aunty Emily in Artisan Place in Heeley, and they were evacuated from their homes for the same reason, except that their particular unexploded bomb was sticking out of a cellar grate on Plantation Road.

Grandma was not with him, and when the reason for this was explained all else was completely forgotten. Grandma, who was a semi-invalid, was unable to go into any shelter during the raid, and Grandpa stayed with her, in the living room of their home. She had been lying on the settee when a bomb dropped nearby, and the blast had caused her to fall from the settee and on to the floor. Her illness was such that her bones were easily broken and consequently, as well as concussion and much bruising, she suffered a broken hip. She needed hospital treatment, and had been taken away in an ambulance during the night, but on making enquiries, no-one could tell Grandpa where she had been taken. Mum and Aunty Alice immediately left everyone to their own devices and set out to find which hospital she was in. They contacted the Emergency Services and were told that the raid had caused many casualties, not as many as first feared, but bad enough by any standards.

The Sheffield hospitals were coping magnificently with the great influx of victims brought in during the night, but at some point could not cope with any more. Many people had been taken to hospitals in other towns in the outlying areas and it was far too early to find out who had gone where. The casualty lists would be distributed as soon as it was humanly possible and they were advised to go home, where they would be informed as soon as these lists were available. It took four days to find Grandma Wilson's whereabouts – she had been taken to the Pinderfield Hospital in Wakefield.

I had two claims to fame during this time. The first was early in 1940 when my friend, Brenda, and I were photographed outside Carterknowle Road School during a gas attack practice. (The picture was in the local paper, but we were completely unrecognisable because we were wearing gas-masks at the time.) The second time was when the casualty lists were posted on the door of the Warden's Post in

Smithywood Road, and there was the name *Wilson, Mrs A.E*, for all to see. No-one else in my group of friends knew anyone whose name was actually on a casualty list, and my sisters and I were regarded with something like awe. I remember taking groups of open-mouthed children, rather like a conducted tour, to look at the list pinned to the wooden door of the Post. Actually, the Warden's Post was the converted cellar of Smithywood Working Men's Club, but it had an impressive bank of sandbags around the entrance. Looking back, it must have been an Air-Raid Warden's dream to have the Wardens' Post in the beer cellar of the local WMC: I remember the whole family going into that particular Post early in 1939, to collect our gas-masks. It must have been just before Easter, because on the way home, carrying one each of these small square boxes, Dad called out to an acquaintance that we had just been for our Easter eggs. That is exactly what they looked like, in their regulation, plain cardboard cartons, but when the war began and it became an offence not to carry one's gas-mask at all times when out of doors, fashionable cases were on sale at any store which sold handbags and shoes. As these gas-masks had to be taken wherever we went during the next few years, there was always a contest going on as to who was sporting the best gas-mask case.

The **Marples Hotel** *on the corner of Fitzalan Square, looking up High Street after the air raid on the night of Thursday 12th December 1940.*

After the Blitz

O
N THE DAY AFTER THE SHEFFIELD BLITZ, daylight brought the full extent of the destruction in the City Centre and elsewhere across the city. Moving around in Sheffield was virtually impossible, as most main roads in and out of the city were littered with burning and burnt-out trams and buses. Many buses and trams had simply been abandoned during the horrors of the raid. Sheffield Moor, from Moorhead to the bottom of Ecclesall Road, was a mass of flames.

In the City Centre, most buildings on Fargate had not been destroyed but only damaged by the blast of the bombs, but on Angel Street and King Street every building had either been destroyed, or was still on fire. The seven-storey building at the corner of Fitzalan Square and High Street was the *Marples Hotel* (which has only recently been rebuilt) and here the city suffered the heaviest casualties of the bombing. This hotel suffered a direct hit at just after 11.30pm, and rescue work was started the following mid-morning. Some survivors were brought out, but the search for the rest of the people, who had been sheltering underneath the hotel during the worst of the raid, was to take weeks rather than days. In all, sixty-four bodies were brought out, only fourteen of which could be positively identified. The other victims could only be identified by items found on the bodies.

Near the Cathedral, in Church Street, the Royal Insurance Building had disappeared under a mass of rubble, although Telephone Buildings, further up West Street, remained untouched. Many of the big department stores which were situated on The Moor were in ruins, and for a long time afterwards some of them were in temporary premises. I remember particularly John Atkinson's opening very quickly from the

Central Picture House just opposite, and John Walsh, where House of Fraser now stands, opened at The Mount at Broomhill and continued trading there until well after my marriage in 1951.

One store opened up again in the *Landsdowne* Picture Palace on London Road. I can't recall which one it was, but I remember going there with Brenda to buy some Christmas cards. Being a cinema, the floor was on a slope, and the counters had been positioned endways on to where the screen had been. They had been constructed in such a way that although they were level in order to prevent the goods from sliding screenwards, the customers were standing on the slope. As children worldwide will know only too well, it is difficult enough to see over a normal counter. To these children I will say, just try it when one end is nearly a foot higher than the other.

I suppose there was a bonus in all this misery for the children of my generation. Out of a total of 154 schools in the city, eight were destroyed and 106 were damaged, which must have posed quite a problem for the Education Department. In the short term of, course, we had to stay at home, but this happy state of affairs could not go on forever, although it was quite a time before things returned to something like normal. I think it was at this time, or it may have been during the first few weeks of the war when evacuation was in full flow, that the appeal went out for stalwart citizens to open up their front rooms, or indeed any under-used room, to a few children at a time plus one harassed teacher for part-time lessons. This was known as home service, and we went to these classes two or three times a week on a part-time basis for quite a few weeks until we could all return to school.

Once I was taught in someone's spare bedroom, sitting on the bed with our backs to the wall, and the teacher sitting on a dressing table stool, happy as Larry. On reflection, although it was a great adventure for us at the time, it must have taken a feat of organisational skill to get each child to each house for the specified time and class. The teachers, who were in the main women, – the men mostly having been called up and gone to war – must have been worked off their feet, literally.

On Sunday 15th December, the city still reeling from the first raid, another six-wave attack was inflicted upon us, and it lasted for another three hours. This time the bombs were dropped mainly on the industrial area in the east end of the city and damage was done to Steel, Peach and Tozer, Brown Bayley's, Hadfields and the English Steel Corporation, all big names in the Sheffield steel industry. Areas of Firth Park and Darnall were also badly damaged that night. Again, thousands of incendiaries, and about 100 high-explosive bombs, plus five parachute mines, were rained down on the city by 66 Heinkels and eleven Dornier bombers.

These raids were obviously meant to break the morale of the citizens of Sheffield and the other big cities, but instead it worked the other way. The thing I remember most about those times was the neighbourliness, and the quiet determination of people, who went about their daily work as usual, to keep cheerful and make the best of things. Workers walked to work until the transport system was sorted out. Shops opened with boards placed over their shattered windows, with the words 'Business as usual' written all over them, and families, particularly the ones who had lost their homes and all their posessions, suffered great hardship until all the services were back to normal, and new accommodation could be found. Most of these families either lived with relatives or in temporary accommodation in Church Halls or Schools, and as all homeless people, suffered accordingly.

Mondays meant only one thing to my mother. Mondays meant wash-days. Neither Hitler nor the fact that we still had some unexpected guests in the house was going to change the habit of a lifetime, and the Monday following the raids was no exception. Water was at a premium – ours had been cut off since the fisrt blitz – and every drop had to be carried from the water tanker which was situated at the Fire Station on Archer Road. I think there must have been some directive or other about the use of water, and I don't think that the washing of clothes was one of the main priorities. The weather must have been several degrees below, because I remember that the road and pavement were like glass from the water used around the Laycock's area to put out the fires, so it wasn't easy, going up and down the road, carrying water in whatever utensils we could find.

I believe it was Grandpa, who had been in the regular army before and during the First World War, and was used to seeing Indian women doing their laundry in the River Ganges, who suggested fetching water from the river. Anyhow, Mum thought this was an excellent idea, and Grandpa and Margaret were dispatched, with the highest possible speed, to the River Sheaf, which ran on its way from Millhouses Park under Archer Road Bridge. They took with them the small tin bath which had been kept in the cellar from our babyhood, for just such an emergency as this. The river was just over the road, across a small field and down a bank, and ran parallel to the railway-line, so it was quite a struggle for them, over the frozen ground, to reach the river, let alone fill the bath. It wasn't very deep in that spot as I remember, it just managed to gurgle over the stones.

I still don't know how they managed, but they struggled in triumphantly with the precious water. We all gathered around and peered into the bath. Mum looked very doubtfully at Grandpa and mentioned that it wasn't very clean, (and that was an understatement) but Grandpa told her cheerfully that, 'We're not going to drink it, lass. Gerrit in't copper and light the gas under it. When you've got some soap powder in you'll not know the difference.' We all acknowledged that Grandpa was the expert when it came to the washing of clothes in river water, so it was poured into the copper and the wash-day proceeded from there. Of course, the clothes never looked the same again, but they had to be worn.

Clothes, like most other things, were in short supply, and clothing coupons had to be tendered for all new clothes and shoes. As these also had to be used for all household linens, they were treated almost like gold dust

HER HUSBAND HAD DOUBTS

JIM'S AFRAID A PART-TIME JOB AND HOUSEWORK MAY BE TOO MUCH FOR ME

I GOT IN A MUDDLE LAST WEEK. I HAD A HUGE WASH TO BOIL

BUT YOU NEEDN'T BOIL, SILLY!

HOW CAN YOU GET THINGS CLEAN IF YOU DON'T?

WITH RINSO YOU SIMPLY SOAK FOR 12 MINUTES. TRY IT NEXT WEEK!

NEXT WEEK

WELL, HERE GOES. WARTIME METHOD HALF THE WATER AND TWO-THIRDS THE RINSO

THEY'RE GRAND! WHO'D HAVE BELIEVED IT!

THAT NIGHT

YOU'RE A MARVEL, DARLING, RUNNING THE HOUSE AND A JOB TOO

THINKS

IMAGINE GETTING PRAISE LIKE THAT ON WASHDAY!

RINSO is a No. 1 soap powder. 3½d. packet, 1 coupon; 7d. packet, 2 coupons

R 3215-805

R. S. Hudson Limited

24

by wartime families. When I first met my husband in 1948 he had just been demobbed from the Navy. Newly demobilised personnel were issued with quite a lot of these coupons, and he gave me enough to buy a new coat and shoes. I was seventeen at the time and the New Look by Christian Dior had arrived from Paris. All dresses and coats were being worn at calf-length that summer, so, if you had the clothing coupons, you could be dressed in the latest fashion. I hadn't any coupons left, so such extravagant gestures were out of the question. I think that the reason I fell for him was because of his clothing coupon allowance, which I used wisely but well.

For a short time after the Blitz, we were forbidden to stray far from home. The grown-ups had the jitters, now that we had received a couple of visits from the Luftwaffe, expecting them to return at any moment and give us more of the same, so we all played locally. It's amazing how children get information so quickly, when sometimes grown-ups are unaware of it, but the day after the first raid the word went round that Woodseats School had been bombed. This was received with great delight from those friends who attended there. (We had started our schooling there, but Mum moved us to Carterknowle at the beginning of the war, because it was nearer to home.)

As bombed buildings at this time were completely alien to us, we set off up Woodseats Road to take a look. There were quite a few damaged homes on this road, and one of them was the house that my paternal Grandparents had lived in prior to their deaths in 1937, and where my father and his brothers and sister had been brought up. It is still obvious today where the house used to be. Most houses in Woodseats Road were ordinary terrace types, with a passage going from the road to the backs of the houses. At the end of these passages, there are usually four houses, two to the right and two to the left, but opposite the bottom of Todwick Road there is the usual passage, but only two houses to the left. Two are missing from that back yard – the two which were on the right. My Grandparents lived in the first one, and in the top one had lived a family named King. The King's house had been completely destroyed and the other house was so badly damaged that it had to be demolished to make safe. I remember feeling quite sad at the sight, for

I always loved to go to Grandma's, mainly because we were allowed to do exactly as we liked in her house, which we were never allowed to do at home. According to Mum, Grandma was not very houseproud, and she never minded if we turned her stool upside down and used it as a boat, or tap-danced on the lino in front of her cellar door, to music from the old sixpenny records which they bought from Woolworths. Tap dancing on the lino at home was almost a hanging offence.

There was always the smell of Grand-dad's twist tobacco, which was bought in a block, and sliced with a pen-knife, and which he always kept on a little table behind the door. If I close my eyes, I can still smell my Grandparents' house, and see the custard-cream biscuits bought from Lipton's, at the top of the Dale, and chosen from a row of clear-topped biscuit tins, arranged in front of the counter, which Grandma always had on the cellar top, just for us. Although a new, modern building, standing nicely back from the road, has been erected in the gap, whenever I go up Woodseats Road I always take a nostalgic look at the house which, so obviously, isn't there.

We carried on to the top of the road to complete our mission, which was originally to view the damage at Woodseats School, but we could only stand on the opposite side of Chesterfield Road, and quite a distance away, because Civil Defence workers were working at the scene. We saw a bit of smoke and a lot of activity, but nothing much to get excited about, so we wandered back home to report on what we had seen. I never quite understood my Mother's logic when I was a child. When I told her about Grandma's house, she said what a blessing it was that they had both died in 1937 or they would probably have been sheltering with the Kings. I remember thinking that I didn't think it a blessing when Grandma died, and they may have been in another shelter, anyway. It was the same sort of logic that she used when the evacuation of children was first mooted at the beginning of the war. 'My kids are going nowhere', she said, 'If we're going to be killed we are all going to go together'. Looking back, I suppose that she was right on both counts, but all I knew then was that I didn't want to die, and I didn't want anyone else to die either.

After a few days, our visitors all returned to their homes, except

Aunty Nellie and Uncle Henry, who were to stay in our front room, sleeping on a bed settee for a few more weeks. Christmas came and went, and the only thing I can really remember about that Christmas was the fact that, for the first and only time, I saw my Father the worse for drink. Mum had gone, with Aunty and Uncle, up to the house at Norton to see if anything could be salvaged from the ruins. Dad was finishing work at lunchtime on Christmas Eve, and I was waiting at the bottom of the passage for him to come home, but he was very late. When he did arrive, he was acting very strangely, and after taking off his coat he tried to sit down in his chair but fell in a big heap on to the floor. I was alone and thought that he had been taken ill again. I helped him to get up, and he eventually managed to find the seat of his chair. By this time, I was almost hysterical, and was running up and down the passage to see if Mum was coming. When she arrived, Dad was snoring happily in his chair, and I was trying to tell her between sobs that Dad had fallen down, and that he was very poorly.

She took one look at him, and said, 'Stop that row, he's not poorly, he's falling-down drunk', and she swept majestically into the kitchen to get the tea ready, and flatly refused to speak to him for the rest of the holiday. That was Mother – no making allowances for the festive season, or for that matter, the fact that we had all come through the greatest danger that we had ever had to face in all our lives.

WARDONIA
BLADES
For Better Shaves

FOOD FACTS

Packed Lunches
for a whole week

*Six suggestions for a packed meal that are tasty,
nourishing and full of variety*

Are you stumped to know what to put into the packed lunches your family take off to work? It *is* a problem.

You don't want to give them the same old thing every day — and it's not good for them, either. People do best on variety, and they need a balance of body-building and energy-giving food, including plenty of protective food, especially greenstuff.

Follow these suggestions. They'll take a load off your mind for a whole week, and they'll make sure the lunches you put up contain proper nourishment.

MONDAY
Sandwiches filled with mixture of cold mashed potato, grated cheese, chutney, and chopped fresh parsley
Lettuce
Jam turnover

TUESDAY
Turnover filled with mixture of chopped cooked beans, melted cheese, and chopped parsley; tomato
Raw cabbage salad in a screw-top jar
Chocolate Pin Wheels

WEDNESDAY
Potato scones filled with scrambled dried eggs, cooked mixed vegetables, and chopped parsley
Watercress
Prune dumplings

THURSDAY
Rissoles made with cooked meat, cooked beans and mashed potato
Raw spinach and lettuce
Fruit turnovers

FRIDAY
Soup
Sandwiches filled with scrambled dried eggs, mashed potato and chopped fried bacon
Radishes or tomatoes
Lettuce

SATURDAY
Turnover filled with sausage meat, cooked dried peas, herbs, parsley, and chopped leek or onion
Raw cabbage salad in a screw-top jar
Oatmeal scones and jam

RATION BOOKS
There is no general re-registration, but you will be able to change a retailer *after August 8th* by applying to the Food Office between August 8th and August 28th. You cannot change your milk retailer.

You may not be able to get all these things where you live, but they are available now in most places. Recipes for any of the above may be had from the Ministry of Food, Portman Square, London, W.1.

**THIS IS WEEK I — THE FIRST WEEK OF
RATION PERIOD No. I (July 25th to August 21st)**

ISSUED BY THE MINISTRY OF FOOD   FOOD FACTS No. 140

School was different, then . . .

THE NEW YEAR OF 1941 dawned, and things on the Home Front began to get back to something approaching normal. After a few weeks, normal school started again, and by the Spring, for the children at least, life went on much as it always had done. With the lighter nights, the whips and tops came out again, together with the skipping ropes and all the other things that children the world over amused themselves with.

In February, I was allowed, for the first time in my life, to take the day off school without the excuse of a sore throat or something worse. I actually got permission from Mr Pears, the Headmaster, to go with Aunty Alice to visit Grandma Wilson in Wakefield. It is over fifty years since that day, but I remember it as if it happened yesterday, mainly because it was the first time in my ten years that I had ever eaten a meal in a restaurant.

We went by bus from Castlegate, and arrived around lunchtime. Aunty wasn't familiar with the eating establishments of Wakefield, but she knew that Woolworth's served food, so that was there we went. It may not be everyone's choice of cuisine, but to me the austerity meal we ate in that café was fit for a king. I looked at Aunty Alice with new eyes from that day on, and decided that she must be awfully rich to eat in places of such splendour.

We arrived at the hospital a little time before visiting, and I recall waiting in a big empty room, with very high windows and double doors. But it was the very highly polished floor that really impressed me. Having 'saved mum a job' a time or two with the Mansion Polish and a soft duster on the lino at home, I couldn't believe how many hours it must have taken, or how many people would be involved in

the polishing of such a wide expanse of floor. It impressed me so much that when I returned home I kept on about it to anyone who would listen, until they got heartily sick of the subject. Mum said that if I was so interested in the subject of polished floors, she would get me a job in service when I was old enough. I declined the offer and went off in a huff, because everyone knew that I had set my heart on being a cinema usherette when I left school,

Grandma wasn't so well when we eventually got in to visit her. The nursing staff had been trying to help her to walk, when she slipped again, (probably on the highly polished floor previously mentioned) and broke her other hip. She was eventually moved to Firvale Hospital in Sheffield, but she never walked again. She spent the next few years until her death in 1944 alternating between Firvale and our front room, where she often stayed, only going back into hospital when Mum needed a rest.

It got so bad eventually, that Mum had to stop Dad from visiting her in the Hospital, because each time he went she wanted so much to come home that Dad couldn't say no to her. Mum tried to point out to him that it wasn't easy coping with everything in wartime, with a family to feed, and having to queue for almost all the basic things in life, and trying to cope with Grandma as well, He agreed, but as I remember, Grandma spent a lot of time with us during those years.

School was very different in those days. Before the war, girls from my age and older were taught domestic science, and boys were taught woodwork. The boys were able to carry on making things out of bits of wood, but there was not the food available for girls to learn how to cook. This proved no hardship for me at all, I never fancied messing about with cooking utensils and ladles, I much preferred a drawing book and a couple of pencils. There was a beautiful Domestic Science lab at Carterknowle, but in my day it was only used for the teachers and the dinner ladies to eat their mid-day meal.

School dinners started about this time, and I was allowed to stay for lunch on Mondays, Wednesdays and Fridays. They were cooked in the kitchens of Abbeydale Grange School, and delivered to Carterknowle in large containers, which looked a little like milk churns. We didn't have such niceties as dining rooms in schools in those days, so we just propped up the lids of our desks with books to make a level surface, and ate in the classroom. Some girls brought little tray cloths and serviettes from home, but Brenda and I scorned such fripperies and put it all down to these girls living at Millhouses and Totley. Speaking for myself, I don't think that we had a tray cloth in the house, and if we had, Mum would never have let me take it to school. Brenda and I were almost inseparable friends for many years. From the day her family moved into the house around the corner, in Woodseats Road, just before the war started, we did everything together. One was very rarely seen without the other, which prompted Mum to ask on more than one occasion, if maybe we were joined at the hip?

Hilda was always in trouble at dinner-time. We had to queue to be served, and the first thing in line were the knives, forks and spoons, in three separate boxes. Hilda was always most particular about everything and, without fail, she would first take out a fork and smell it, and if it didn't suit she would put it back until she found one that did. This procedure went on until she had a satisfactory set of cutlery, and it always infuriated the teacher in charge. Most days she was sent to the end of the queue, but she still continued to do it. I once asked her why, and she just said that she couldn't eat her lunch with cutlery which smelled fishy. As most days it *did*, I couldn't really argue with her.

I always enjoyed these school dinners, that is, except the one which had beetroot as the vegetable. I hated the way the juice from the beetroot would mingle with the gravy, and then seep into the mashed potato. I always thought it the most revolting mess ever to appear on a dinner plate.

Sewing and knitting also almost disappeared from the school curriculum. Miss Doxey was the teacher in our particular class, and she tried very hard to provide us with some sort of material, but it was never easy. The only knitting yarns available were of a very poor quality and very hard on the hands, and material for sewing was rationed, like most other things at the time. However, one day she came into the classroom with a few yards of pale blue winceyette which she had procured, to make some pyjamas. She thought it a good idea in the circumstances to have them made in class, and she chose her two star sewers to make them. Brenda and I could never understand where she had got the idea that we were the best sewers in the class, we just assumed that she had had a rush of blood to the head. So under her eagle eye we proceeded to cut and sew her precious material. Brenda was elected to do the bottoms, and I to make the top. I don't know exactly how long we took to make those pyjamas, but it felt like years. As they progressed, they seemed to assume gigantic proportions, and we were often in fits of laughter (when she wasn't looking, of course) trying to imagine our Miss Doxey, who was quite the most prim and proper lady that we had ever seen, getting into her bed and wearing our handiwork, which would probably have been too large for King Kong.

Miss Doxey took all aspects of the war very seriously, and during the 'Dig for Victory' campaign, she arrived one day with some packets of seeds. Sharing them out methodically, one packet between two pupils, she marched us outside to the only patch of earth available in the vicinity. This was at the top of the infants' playground, where the air raid shelters were situated. These shelters were covered with earth, and here we were going to have the most magnificent vegetable garden in the whole of the City – she said.

Brenda and I had the packet with radishes on the front, so naturally, we assumed that if we put the seeds into the earth we would get rows of radishes eventually. We would have preferred something else, maybe a lettuce, or a few carrots, but we got the radishes. When I was at school, arguing with the teacher was not recommended, so we set to and prepared the ground, or rather, we dug a bit with a trowel which had been provided by the Caretaker along with a few more gardening implements, and we sowed the seeds. Every day we would go up to the shelters, and water our precious seeds, inspecting the lumpy ground for any trace of the culinary sights to come, but nothing ever appeared. Not one radish ever graced our table, nor one vegetable ever graced anyone else's; the whole project had been a complete failure and it put me completely off gardening for life.

Gas mask drill was also taken very seriously by Miss Doxey. Occasionally we actually had to sit at our desks and take lessons wearing them. They were made of a stretchy kind of rubber, and were pulled on, fitting very snugly beneath the chin and over the front of the head. There was a piece of celluloid at eye level which always misted up after the mask had been worn for a few minutes, and this posed great problems when trying to read or write whilst wearing one. One girl imparted the news that if the eye-piece was rubbed over with soap before use, it didn't steam up, so, before the next drill, everyone in the class rubbed the eye-piece over with soap. We didn't steam up, but no-one could see a thing through them, either, so the drill was cancelled.

After Dunkirk, the country became so involved with the Battle of Britain, and the horrors of the air raids, that the events taking place in other parts of the world, particularly in the Mediterranean, went almost unnoticed.

In 1936 the fascist dictator of Italy, Benito Mussolini, had overrun Abyssinia, and in March 1939 had done the same to Albania, both easy victories against two weaker countries. On 10th June 1940 he declared war on France and Britain. Old Musso, as we kids called him, was yet another comic-opera kind of man. Fat, pompous, always strutting around with his nose in the air, and his considerable amount of chin sticking out. But in addition to all this, he had delusions of grandeur, and far beyond his capabilities. I once read somewhere that, 'Rarely has one man's pride led so consistently to disaster for his countrymen, as Mussolini's did for the Italians.'

In August, Italy announced the total blockade of Britain's Mediterranean and African possessions, and in October, Italian forces streamed over the Albanian border into Greece. But Greece was no pushover for the Italians as Abyssinia and Albania had been, and by 8th December 1940, with British help, the

Italians were pushed back into Albania. But on 6th April 1941, Germany invaded Greece, and after much bitter fighting by the Greek and British forces, the British evacuated their last remaining men at the end of April 1941, and it was all over. Greece became yet another occupied territory.

All these events in the Mediterranean meant that Malta was now struggling for her survival. After the Italians dropped their first load of bombs on the island, a few hours after entering the war in June 1940, Malta was constantly bombarded by the combined might of Italy and Germany for the next three years.

Meanwhile, a new name was being bandied about in the neighbourhood. The Desert Fox, or to give him his correct name, General-Lieutenant Erwin Rommel flew into Tripoli in North Africa, on 12th February 1941. He was destined to become the most famous German soldier of the Second World War.

All this meant little or nothing in the schoolyard. Some of the boys would play games, some on the side of Rommel and others on the side of the British, but Rommel's lot always got the pummelling, so they soon tired of it, and went back to playing the old familiar cowboys and Indians.

Two more events happened in 1941, which changed the course of the war. In June, to everyone's amazement, Germany invaded Russia. This was greeted with complete disbelief by every grown-up around us. Nearly everyone at that time had at least recognised the possibility that the Germans may invade England early that summer, and then the news broke that they had gone the other way and invaded on an Eastern Front. My Dad thought that, at last, Hitler had completely lost his marbles. So now we had an ally. Russia was now at war with Germany, and Communist country or no, it was a very big country to have on our side.

Then, in December 1941, the Japanese made a surprise air attack on the American fleet at Pearl Harbour, and President Roosevelt declared war on Japan and the Axis forces in Europe (for that was the name used to describe the enemy, just as the people who were fighting with us were called the Allies). The United States were now in the war, and the three countries – Russia, America and Britain – started to plan the strategy that would lead, after almost four more years of bitter fighting, to the downfall of the Third Reich, and the end of the Second World War.

But, until that happy day, occupied Europe was to suffer appallingly under the jackboot of the Nazis. The Gestapo, well-known in Germany since the early 'thirties, was to rear its even uglier head as an occupying force. They were the hated State Police, always portrayed in the films of that era as men wearing leather coats and dark trilby hats. They always walked around in twos, and looked extremely sinister.

Although this description was partly true, in reality they were very dangerous men, wedded to the State and their doctrine, and they carried out their duties cruelly and efficiently, in France, Belgium and Holland, and all the other countries under Nazi domination. So it is not surprising that in most of these lands opposition grew and resistance groups began to spring up all over Europe, many of them secretly armed by the Allies. By June 1944, when the invasion took place, there were thousands of patriots waiting eagerly to help in the liberation of their countries.

But we children didn't know about any of these things. As long as the sun was shining or the snow was falling, we were content to pass our time doing what all children do best, living life to the full, and leaving all the unimportant things to the grown-ups.

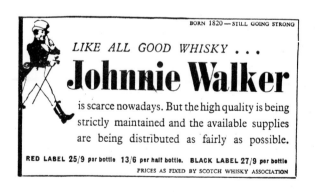

Normal, healthy children

O N REFLECTION, some of the exploits enjoyed by Brenda and I could have jumped out of the pages of any *Just William* book. The one that springs immediately to mind is when we gatecrashed a Sunday School party. We seemed to wander all over the place when we were kids, not particularly looking for mischief, but often finding it nevertheless. We often walked down to Highfield Library on a Saturday, and on one of these trips, as we were passing Abbeydale Congregational Church we noticed a poster outside which informed passers-by that there was in progress a Christmas Fayre, after which the Sunday School Party would take place.

During the war there was never much in the way of party fare to be had, and being two normal, healthy children, the opportunity of anything out of the ordinary to eat proved too much of a temptation to be ignored. We carried on down to the library, perfecting our master plan on the way. Just before the appointed time the party was due to start, we wandered nonchalantly into the Church Hall and looked around the stalls with studied interest. Most of the goods had already been sold by this time, which was perhaps just as well, we very rarely had a penny piece between the two of us. Come to think of it, this was always the main reason for walking down to Highfield Library every Saturday; we never had the money for the tram.

Down one part of the room, trestle tables were being covered by cloths, and quite a few children were helping, so we just joined in. With commendable enthusiasm, we fetched and carried the plates of potted meat and shrimp-paste sandwiches (there were a lot of those about during the War), and cakes and buns, placing them with mathematical precision down the centre of the tables. Small plates were arranged down each side, and jugs and cups were strategically placed at each end. We worked extremely hard, and when all was ready we merely slipped on to the end of one of the long wooden benches, and tucked in with the rest of them.

I still don't understand to this day how we managed to get away with it without being rumbled, and even after all these years I still feel guilty about the whole episode. At the time, of course, guilt was not a word which featured much in our vocabulary. The fact that the very enjoyable feast was provided with great dedication – and probably greater sacrifices from the meagre rations of many a worthy church lady – bothered us not one jot. Had the same opportunity presented itself on some future occasion, no doubt we would have again taken full advantage of the situation. If we had any thoughts on the matters – apart from the obvious childish one that God should feed everybody anyway – it wasn't that we were being a trifle dishonest, but rather that we were being tremendously resourceful. After all, we were in our own way preserving our families' scanty food supplies at home. But we knew that our mothers would not have viewed the matter in quite the same way, and we decided on the way home that maybe it would be more expedient not to say anything about it.

It was about this time that I made an amazing discovery. Not earth-shattering in the general sense, but it meant a lot to me. I realised that, after years of trying, I was able to whistle.

It goes without saying that not everyone was as delighted with my prowess as I was. In fact, two people – my mother and a very irate gentleman in the Doctor's waiting room – were positively antagonistic. Mum had very set ideas on quite a number of topics: politics, Hitler, Lord Woolton, wasting valuable time reading comics and trashy books, and many more, but she had a particular aversion to whistling females. Whenever I launched into one of my ear-piercing tunes she would glare and recite one of her stack of appropriate maxims. 'A whistling woman and a crowing hen, will bring the devil out of his den.' This was usually enough to shut me up and consequently I practised most of my tunes out of doors.

One day I was sent down to Dr Atkinson's surgery to pick up a prescription for Uncle Ted. The waiting room was a very boring place to spend what seemed to me like hour, and after inspecting the walls and the ceiling for a while, I turned my attention to the waiting patients. No-one spoke, no-one smiled, they just sat there, arranged around the room on their hard wooden chairs like so many zombies, and they all looked as miserable as I was. So I withdrew into my own little world and began to whistle a few tunes.

I was completely oblivious to the effect my repertoire was having upon these unfortunate victims, until I was brought back to reality with a bump. An elderly man was poking my foot with his walking stick and informing me in no uncertain terms that he'd never heard such a row in all his life, and that if he knew who my father was he would go straight round to see him. Fortunately, the doctor brought out Uncle Ted's prescription just then, and I made my escape as quickly as possible. I remember noticing on my way out that the remaining patients had perked up considerably. There's nothing like a good old harangue to dispel boredom, but I must admit to feeling a little aggrieved about the incident. After all, we were always being encouraged over the radio to keep our chins up and be cheerful, and as I walked home, I reasoned that I had at least done my bit on that particular day to considerably help the war effort.

There was no National Health Service when we were children, that didn't start till 1947. All visits to and from the Doctor and all medicines were charged for. Mum would pay a few coppers each week to a man who called on behalf of the Doctor on Friday evenings, and who was referred to by one and all, as 'the Doctor's Man'.

Consequently the doctor was only called upon in a dire emergency, and home remedies were heavily relied upon. One that I particularly remember was the old baking tins filled with tar on the oven top. Hilda and I both had whooping cough at the same times and the tar – begged from the road menders somewhere in the vicinity, and kept hot near the stove – had to be inhaled each time we started to cough.

Sore throats were always treated with a vinegar-and-water gargle, and when Mum had a headache, lying down in a darkened room with cloths soaked in vinegar on her forehead, followed by a quick rub with a melrose stick (a menthol-smelling solid, which was dispatched from a tube in the manner of today's Pritstick) was the order of the day.

Sal Volatale was used in copious amounts by Grandma for her heart flutters, and a few crystals of Permanganate of Potash were always dropped into the water on bath nights as an antiseptic. After bathing we all received a quick flick through the hair with a small-toothed comb, for Mum was always on the lookout for nits, but they seemed to give our house a wide berth (I don't think they would have dared), and this was often followed by a spoonful of 'Brimstone and Treacle ' if required for the proper functioning of the internal system. As we left for school each morning, a spoonful of Parrish's Chemical food was administered as we walked out of the door. I was never sure why, but Mum obviously thought that it was a good idea at the time, and at the first indication of a cold, the Fennel or quinine bottle, depending on the severity of the symptoms, was brought down from the top shelf of the cupboard.

Most of the kids at school smelled strongly of Wintergreen ointment, which was spread liberally on 'bad chests' during the winter months, and sometimes goose grease – which smelled even worse – was used for the same purpose, but Mum drew the line at that.

No, the Doctor wasn't a frequent visitor in most homes when we were children, for he cost money and there wasn't much of that around.

Concerts were an integral part of our childhood. Not the official kind, but rather the home-grown variety, which would usually take place in backyards or in the field which backed on to the houses on our side of the road. When the weather warmed up a bit, the children in our road and surrounding areas could often be seen taking part in one of these impromptu performances. Cupboards and rag bags were raided in the search for suitable bits and bobs to dress up in, and many a piece of old net curtaining was spirited away from under the very noses of our unsuspecting mothers. As I recall, knicker legs were by far the most successful hiding places for borrowed items.

The Post Office sorting office yard in Woodseats Road was one of the best venues for a concert. The loading platform provided a ready-made stage, and a grassy bank along the front of it was almost custom-built for the audience. The gates were locked after the day's work, and the whole area was deserted for the evening. The surrounding high walls – presumably built to keep out burglars – didn't prove much of a deterrent to groups of determined children bent on spending an hour or so in the pursuit of happiness, but we only used it very occasionally. We all knew that we were trespassing and that we shouldn't be in there, and it became a bit of a drag having to keep a weather eye open for the return of a stray member of staff, or the helmet of a passing policeman, bobbing up and down beyond the wall.

One day, toward the end of the long summer holidays, rumour had it that one of the lads down the road was going to do a parachute jump out of his back bedroom window. There would be a small charge of one halfpenny to watch him do it, and seating would be provided. Now normally we didn't take a lot of notice of the boasting of small boys, but this was different. The lad in question had quite a reputation for being a little daredevil, and after much earnest discussion we were all of the unanimous opinion that, if he said he was going to jump, then he was going to jump. We deliberated again as to whether it would be worth a halfpenny, and it was decided that under the circumstances it would be jolly good value for money.

Consequently, quite a crowd of us poured into his backyard that afternoon, paid over our entrance fee, and took our seats on a variety of stools, upturned buckets, bricks and upturned plant pots. We waited expectantly, all eyes fixed firmly on the slightly opened spare room window, over the passage, until he appeared.

It was all a big let-down, of course. He *did* climb out on to the window sill, where he sat for five minutes or so, clutching an opened umbrella, but he didn't jump, and – to a chorus of cat-calls, and as near as we could get to cries of derision – disappeared back inside.

We eventually got our money back. There were too many of us, and he knew that he couldn't fight us all, but after that day he was a fallen idol (but not literally), and we never believed another word he said.

A wartime Christmas

T THE START OF 1942, war was raging in almost every corner of the world, and faraway places were becoming household names. The Japanese forces in China had attacked the British Colony of Hong Kong only four hours after its attack on Pearl Harbour. By Christmas Day, the British Garrison on the Island had surrendered, and the two battleships *Repulse* and *Prince of Wales* were at the bottom of the Pacific Ocean. On February 7th, the Japanese landed large forces on Singapore Island, and by February 15th, after fierce and bitter fighting the British surrendered.

As children, we were always being advised to be seen and not heard, so I had become very skilled at eavesdropping. As the conversation of the grown-ups, at every gathering, was mainly about the War, the events in the Far East were very surprising to me. I had heard many times over the preceeding months that we had little to fear from the Japanese. After all, it was a well-documented fact, Mum said, that Japanese soldiers rode into battle on bicycles, and wore only plimsolls on their feet, not good army boots like our lads. Dad would nod wisely and add that the Japs had a whole lot of tanks made completely of cardboard, so that, when seen from the air, it would make the Allies think that they were better equipped than they really were.

As for Singapore – well, everyone knew that Singapore was a virtual fortress, with all those great big guns pointing out to sea, and all that impenetrable jungle to the rear. No-one could possibly invade from the rear, especially on bicycles and wearing plimsolls – no, there would be nothing to fear from the Japs. But as it turned out, of course, there was plenty to fear from them, and events would disprove the notion that we had nothing to fear from the Japs.

Whilst all this was going on in the world, I had plenty of smaller troubles of my own. The Scholarship was looming very near. This was the name of the examination – later known as the Eleven Plus – which was abandoned altogether in the 1960s, in favour of the Comprehensive System.

This was the time for all teachers to inform most of the pupils in junior schools, that if they didn't work much harder they wouldn't have a hope of passing the Scholarship, and would most probably be cast out into the wilderness, without a prayer of getting a Decent Job. All the Decent Jobs, according to Miss Doxey, were in banking or the Civil Service, unless of course, one was clever enough to go to College, and then the world could be one's oyster. This went completely over my head, because none of these careers appealed to me in the slightest. All I wanted to do, in those days, was to be a Cinema Usherette. The joy of seeing all those glamorous stars, and all those films, without paying a penny piece to go in, was my idea of heaven, for at ten years old I wasn't very ambitious! But, even in spite of my modest aspirations when it was time to go out into the wide world, I still had to take the Scholarship examination.

It was taken in two parts, the first in February and the second in March, and we obtained the results in late July or early August. Brenda and I had worked it all out, that if we entered the same choice of school on the official form, and the same second choice, we would be sure to be able to stay together. This plan completely depended on both of us getting a pass. But, as the well-known saying goes, 'The best laid plans of mice and men . . .' etc, and we finished up at different schools.

I remember well the first term at my new school. It was the most miserable time of my life. Everything was so different. Instead of being a big fish in a little pond (as we were in the senior class at Carterknowle), I was now a very small minnow, in a very large lake. I didn't know anyone, and no-one knew me. The teachers were mostly elderly men and (it seemed to me) even older ladies, and, in my first year, the form master we were landed with was the biggest bore in the world. He would lean on the wall at one side of the classroom, swinging the cane, with his eyes closed, and drone on and on, then suddenly, when we least expected it, he would leap into action brandishing the cane in the air, and threatening the whole class with all kinds of physical violence. We were convinced that, because of the extreme shortage of teachers at that time, he had been released from the looney-bin for the duration.

Actually, it transpired that he was an extremely clever man, but I can honestly say that he didn't teach me very much. I spent much of the time gazing out of the window, and day dreaming. Fortunately, we had different teachers for different subjects, so we spent much of our time traipsing from class to class and building to building, in search of the teacher who was named on our timetable.

Sometimes the aforesaid teacher failed to turn up, and then the Headmaster would appear to inform us that we could spend the time revising for the next session, and as we were now regarded as responsible children, who should be able to work without supervision, he would leave us alone to do exactly that. He was a lovely man, our Headmaster, very fair and kind-hearted, and we always tried to do as he asked, but I felt that he was far too trusting, especially whilst I was trying to dodge one of the ink-soaked pieces of paper which the lads would start to catapult around the room before he had barely closed the door.

In time, of course, I settled down, made a host of new friends, and began to enjoy my new life. Brenda and I remained the best of friends, out of school for the rest of our schooldays, and indeed, until we met our future husbands. Strangely enough, we were later to get married on the same day, quite accidentally, not by design.

We went through a lot together. The traumas of broken hearts, which all teenagers suffer, and all the other discoveries connected with growing up. Our favourite pastime during the summer months, particularly during the long summer holidays, was to take advantage of the 'Holidays at Home' programmes in all the Sheffield parks. There was always a concert or a dance (I wouldn't recommend ballroom dancing on grass, but we used to have a wonderful time) in one of the parks around the neighbourhood, and we would visit them all.

The concerts were a great source of amusement. There was always a duet, usually a very large lady, in a long frilly frock which had obviously seen better days, accompanied by a bald-headed tenor with a face like a frog. At every concert they would sing, either *Because*, *If you would give me the key to your heart* or *Trees*. Sometimes, if the comic had failed to turn up, we got the lot. But the thing that really got us almost crying with laughter was the way the very large lady would run a chiffon scarf through her fingers, almost in anguish, as she strained to reach the high notes. We once got thrown out of the roped-off area during one of those hilarious duets.

In Millhouses Park, in front of the Recreation Hut, there used to be a very large chess board, and Brenda and I spent hours on there, moving great hulking draughts around, with a pole with a hook on the end. The elderly gentlemen for whom the pastime was intended would sit around the board on the seats provided, giving us advice and generally teaching us the game. We became quite proficient eventually. By the side of this board lay the tennis courts, and, if funds were high, we would go on for a game. We had absolutely no idea how to score, and we would airily call out, 'Fifteen, love; twenty, love; twenty-five, love,' and so on. Well, we knew it was something like that, but I can well remember the funny looks that we received from people passing by.

We didn't receive pocket money as such, but we often received bits and pieces from Aunts and Uncles, and I used to go shopping for neighbours occasionally and receive a copper or two for my trouble, but this was not enough for our needs, so Brenda and I became very resourceful. Apart from collecting empty bottles and taking them back to the shops, we found out about a shop on London Road which actually paid out money for old magazines. This lovely little shop funded most of our activities for a very long time, for Brenda's mum was an avid magazine reader, and Aunty Alice always had one or two lying around. Yes, we had quite a bit of pocket money from that shop.

During the late summer and Autumn of 1941, after the German army had invaded Russia, they were slicing through towards Moscow at an alarming rate. At school we were learning of faraway Russian towns and cities with very strange names which in normal times, we may never have heard. Brest Livosk, Minsk, Kharkov, Smolensk and many others, all German victories. Kiev was the greatest military disaster in the Red Army's history, and the siege of Leningrad, where thousands of its citizens starved to death during the following winter, began on 15th September 1941.

We learned much about the world in our Geography lessons during the next four years. In the Middle East, great battles were fought in places with strange-sounding names. Sidi Barrani and Benghazi, Tobruk and El Alamein, and in the Far Fast, locations like Wake Island, Corregidor, Bataan and Midway were all scenes of heavy fighting, both on land and at sea.

The almost immediate effect of America's entry into the War was the arrival of the American GI to these shores. This event was given a mixed reception by the British populace, depending mainly on the sex of the person. Most of the young, unattached ladies, and indeed – according to Mum – same of the attached ones as well, greeted them with open arms. The GIs came into Sheffield for socialising, particularly to the *Grand Hotel* and Nell's Bar on Cambridge Street. British men, however, viewed their arrival quite differently. 'Over-paid, over-sexed and over here', was how they phrased it.

The GIs certainly had a lot going for them at the time. After over two years of the War, and the shortages the country had suffered, not to mention the absence of most of our younger men away fighting in the Services, these smartly-uniformed American soldiers, with their apparently unlimited supply of nylon stockings and other luxury goods, must have seemed like manna from Heaven to the young female population of these islands. For myself, I was too young to have any opinion at all, but the dire warnings from Mother, directed towards Margaret, must have rubbed off on me, because whenever I went into town, even after I had left school, and I saw a group of American soldiers, I would cross over the road rather than walk past them. Mother could always instil the fear of God into me.

Looking back, I don't suppose they were any worse, or any better, than any other young men far away from home, probably for the first time. Most of them were quite ordinary, little more than boys really, and many of them married English girls. Two acquaintances of our family did exactly that, and as far as I know have never regretted it, and made new and happy lives for themselves in the United States. Of course, many of them didn't marry, but left fatherless children and crying mothers behind them when they sailed away into the sunset, never to be heard of again.

The advertising hoardings over the war years, were always full of slogans, *Careless Talk Costs Lives, Dig For Victory, 'Coughs And Sneezes Spread Diseases, Trap Those Germs In Your Handkerchief'*, and my favourite, *Be Like Dad, Keep Mum*. All very laudable, and as children we took them almost at face value. I was always on the lookout for spies, in a black flowing cloak, and probably with a round black object tucked under his arm with the word 'BOMB' clearly written on it – spies were always depicted looking like this in the comic books of the time – who would wait, with baited breath, to hear my slightest utterance. But over the next few months, another slogan appeared, written graffiti-style, on buildings and bridges, or anywhere which could be reached by the writer, *Start the Second Front Now*, which roughly translated meant 'start the invasion of Europe now'. But that wasn't to happen until June 1944, and until that time, we still had a long way to go. But at least things were definitely to take a turn for the better during 1943, and morale was high.

Uncle Bill was Dad's elder brother. When he returned from the First World War, he brought with him a new wife, whom he met and married whilst stationed near Reading. This didn't go down very well in some quarters of the family, mainly because he was already walking out with another young lady before he marched off to war, and, in Grandma's words, they had 'an understanding'.

Understanding or no, Uncle Bill arrived home with Aunty Phyllis, a quiet, gentle lady, who did her best to settle in the North. They had one daughter, Joyce, but during the Depression in the 1920s, Uncle Bill could find no work, so they packed their bags, and, taking six-year-old Joyce with them, they went down South, to Portsmouth, where Aunty Phyllis had a brother in the Police Force, and Uncle Bill got a job in the Naval Dockyard.

Mum was very fond of Joyce, and always kept in touch with them, and as she was growing up, she would write letters to us. But as children we had never met her. At the outbreak of war, Joyce joined the WRNS – the Women's Royal Naval Service, which everyone called the Wrens – and during the summer of 1942 she came up to Sheffield on a visit. We thought she was wonderful. She took Hilda and I to the pictures one afternoon and we had a great time. I can even remember the film we saw, so the day must have made a big impression on me. It was *Down Argentina Way* and we travelled to the *Coliseum*, a small cinema at the bottom of Spital Hill, in order to see it. This was a great treat for us, going to the pictures in our best clothes with this very smart young woman in Naval uniform. She stayed with us for a few days until her leave was over, and we waved her off at Midland Station with tears flowing copiously.

I remember one afternoon during her visit, she had been out with Margaret, and they returned to find Brenda and I painting our legs, not with leg paint, (which, because of the acute shortage of stockings, could be bought from any chemist's shop and was used all the time by the older girls) but with paint from my Reeves paint box. Margaret was horrified, and threatened to tell Mum when she came home. We were just about to launch into one of our frequent sisterly punch-ups, when Joyce said gently that we were doing no harm, and Mum need never know if we washed it off. So another good hiding was averted, for Mum wouldn't have leg paint in the house, because she said it went all over the sheets, and The Lord knew, washing powder was difficult enough to obtain without having to use extra to get that muck off the bedding. So, when Joyce went back to Portsmouth I felt that I had lost a friend who understood eleven-year-olds much better than mothers and older sisters did, and I was convinced that I would never see her again. I knew that she only lived on the south coast, but the south coast was nearly as far away as Outer Mongolia as far as I was concerned, and the day that she went home was one of blackest days in my short life.

I remember Christmas 1942 very well. That was the year that a friend of Uncle Ted's promised to supply him with a duck for Christmas dinner. Christmas fare in those days was mainly a matter of what could be saved from the rations during the previous few weeks, rather than anything extra which could be purchased just because it was Christmas. If anything special could be obtained, that was a bonus, and in this case the duck was a bonus, to be enjoyed by all of us. As the great day approached, we awaited the arrival of the promised fowl with almost baited breath, and on Christmas Eve Uncle Ted brought it home.

To be fair, it wasn't a very big duck, even with it's feathers on, and when it had been plucked it was even smaller. By the time it appeared on the dinner table there was hardly enough meat on it for two, never mind seven, but we all had a mouthful or two, and filled up with vegetables. The complainers were reminded, as usual, that people in Europe and elsewhere in the world had to manage on far less, and that we must be grateful for small mercies. As I was one of the loudest complainers, I felt suitably chastised, but I remember thinking that, if Uncle Ted's friend had had to risk life and limb to procure this Christmas repast, surely he could have at least provided a slightly bigger duck.

I can never think of those wartime Christmases without remembering Uncle Ted. He was such an integral part of the festivities, good-humoured always, and with a type of nervous energy which I have never seen in anyone either before or since. He and Aunty Alice loved dancing, and he had the first radiogram I ever saw, which could accommodate more than one record at the same time. But the thing I remember most was Uncle Ted's complete inability to hold his beer. Dad, who could drink anyone under the table at any given time once remarked, that 'Ted had only got to have a sniff at the barman's apron and he was well away'. He drank very little normally, but at all the Christmas parties we ever had, after the first half-pint he would regale us, one and all, with his very own rendition of *The Green Eye of The Little Yellow God*. Arms flailing and eyes rolling, completely ignoring the pleas of Aunty Alice to 'Sit down, for God's sake, Ted', he would dramatically carry on to the bitter end, until his three young nieces were almost hysterical, and often rolling about the floor, doubled up with laughter. We had a lot of fun with Uncle Ted, and the strange think was that most of the time he *was* being a funny man he didn't really mean to be.

By this time the citizens of Leningrad were in the grip of the cruel Russian winter and a siege that was to last for 900 days. Meanwhile, the Germans were racing towards Moscow, but Hitler, as Napoleon before him, had not reckoned on the ferocity of the Russian winter, and his troops and tanks became bogged down in the mud, and were held up for weeks. By mid-November they were battling, not only with the Red Army, but with twenty degrees of frost as well, and they turned for home on December 5th.

In the Western Desert in late June 1942, Rommel took Tobruk, and with his Afrika Korps surged on towards El Alamein. General Montgomery was now the new British desert commander, and during October and the beginning of November, the British Eighth Army – now universally known as the Desert Rats – fought the Battle of El Alamein. It was a great victory, and for the people of Britain this first resounding success, coming in the wake of the first thousand-bomber raid on Cologne on May 31st – which most of the population thought of as 'Giving them a taste of their own medicine' – was a great morale-booster.

As 1942 ended and the New Year of 1943 was about to start, most of the grown-ups around us really felt that the tide had finally begun to turn, and there was now a glimmer of light at the end of the very dark tunnel.

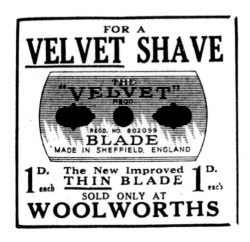

Summer days

A S THE NEW YEAR OF 1943 got under way, Brenda and I joined the Youth Club which had opened on Abbeydale Road. Normally I would not have been allowed to join such an organisation, as Mum held very strong views about such places, and dismissed them all as dens of iniquity, barely one step removed from Sodom and Gomorrah. But, as she knew personally the gentleman in charge of this venture, she didn't think that we would come to any harm, and I was allowed to attend. I often thought later that her faith was quite touching, because, as any twelve-year-old knows, the gentleman in question could never be in all places at all times. But it was all innocent fun and we went there at every opportunity.

It was here that we discovered that even twelve-year-old hearts could be broken – well, perhaps not really, but it felt like it at the time. We learned how to dance properly, to records from the big bands of the day: Glen Miller, the Dorsey's, Benny Goodman, Joe Loss and all the others, which led, as we grew older, to the natural transition across the road to the *Abbeydale* Ballroom, where we spent many happy hours during our early teens.

On Saturday mornings we often went to the *Playhouse Theatre* on Campo Lane, where special junior dances were held for a while during the early part of the year, and sometimes we fulfilled Mum's worst nightmares, and actually met boys. This was definitely not allowed, and many were the times that we hid behind walls or in shop doorways when we espied a neighbour or an acquaintance, who would be likely to tell Mum that we had been seen talking to the lads. How times have changed!

It was around that time that wartime school-yard jokes were beginning to appear. I once repeated one to Mum, and got a clip round the ear for my trouble. I could never understand why she reacted in that way, it didn't seem too bad to me. All I asked her was, did she know where Ghandi kept his fountain pen? I was unsure myself of the exact meaning of this joke, so really I was expecting her to explain it to me. From her reaction I had to presume that it was something very risqué, but the only thing I could think of was that he only ever wore a loin-cloth, and being a statesman, he was bound to have to sign things. As there was very little likelihood of a loin-cloth having a pocket, then he probably had to keep his pen up his knicker leg. I could see no wrong in this solution, because girls of my generation did it all the time, and even to this day I still don't understand what the joke was all about.

During this time, the War was raging fiercely in almost every part of the world. The Allies were fighting the Japanese in the Pacific, and from August 1942 the American Marines were engaged in bitter combat with the Japanese. Losses on both sides in the first six months were heavy, and led to Japan's first land defeat.

Meanwhile, in the Middle East, after the successful battle for Tunisia, the Allies became masters of the North African shores. The invasion of Sicily followed in July, with the collapse of Fascism in Italy soon after. But as German troops poured into Northern Italy and the Allies landed in the South, the battle for Italy began in earnest.

On the Eastern front, the greatest tank battle in history was being waged at Kursk, where armies one million strong on either side endured fierce and stubborn fighting for 15 days, before the Germans were defeated. But the greatest victory of all had been at Stalingrad in January 1943, when the entire German 6th Army surrendered to the Russian General Zhukov. The Battle for Stalingrad, which had cost the Germans one-third of a million men, was over. The Nazi war machine was beginning to crack around the edges.

January 1944 was the month of my thirteenth birthday, but I don't remember a birthday party, we didn't have them during the War. I was now into my teens, a time I had long looked forward to. It had been snowing heavily, as indeed it usually does on my birthday, so we got the sledge out. No store-bought toboggans for us when we were kids. If you had a handy Dad or other male relative, then you were the proud possessor of a sledge. If not, then you stood on the side-lines and begged a ride on someone else's. We had a handy Dad. Well – he was a bit handy, but sometimes things went a bit wrong. Like the time when he built the most beautiful rabbit hutch that we had ever seen. It stood on legs, and had two spacious compartments, one for these lucky rabbits to live in, and one for them to sleep in. It was sturdy, and it was water-proof and altogether the finest hutch in all the street. But, he built it in the cellar, and when it was time to take it outside, it was too big to get it round the corner and up the cellar steps, and it had to be dismantled and rebuilt out of doors.

As we got older, we christened him Uncle Podger, after the charac-ter in *Three men in a boat*, because whenever he did a job, he had all three of us standing around in case he needed anything passing. One to hold the steps, another to pass him the hammer, another the nails and so on. He was once asked if he was ever sorry that he hadn't had a son. 'No, never,' he replied. 'I wouldn't be without my three lasses'.

He made us a lovely sledge. It wouldn't have collapsed if a tank had rolled over it, and there was plenty of room on it for two. The runners were made from bed laths, and it flew like the wind. Our favourite run was down Cartmell Road, the bottom part having a fairly long slope, and here we would spend hours, getting the slope nice and shiny so the sledges could rocket away down the road. We often crossed Ulverston Road, which ran across the bottom, and would finish up in the passage opposite. This would be dangerous in the extreme today, with all the traffic about, but in those days, all we had to worry about was the coal cart, and we usually knew when that was due, because one or all of us had to stay indoors to count the sacks as they were tipped down the cellar grate. No-one seemed to trust the poor old coalman at all.

Sometimes, when we had been careering merrily down the road for ages, perhaps for days, an elderly lady would appear from the house about halfway up on the right, with a shovelful of ashes, and she would make her way precariously across the sledge run, sprinkling the ashes as she went.

This was a sign that the coal cart was due, and the sledging had to stop, otherwise the poor old horse would be unable to get up the hill. We would mumble a bit, but then we would go further afield, to find another run. This was usually Aukley Road, another fine hill, although we weren't so popular with the residents there. But we usually got away with it for a time before we were told to go and play where we belonged, or until the hot-aches in our fingers and toes became too much even for us. At which time we would wander home, and into the warmth, where Mum would be waiting with the hot cocoa.

The fireguard would be festooned with a variety of damp knickers and even damper long black woollen stockings. These monstrosities were the bane of our lives as we were growing up, and had to be worn at all times during the winter months, and indeed until Whitsuntide, when white winter legs were allowed the freedom of white cotton ankle socks. This was particularly hard on Hilda. She had very thin legs as a child, and the black stockings would fall in wrinkles all the way down her legs. This was when she received the nickname of 'Concertina Legs', bestowed on her by Aunty Alice, and which stayed with her throughout her childhood.

For my birthday, I was presented with my very first pair of bedroom slippers, from Mum and Dad. They were brown and white check, with brown pom-poms on the front, and had been purchased from Uncle Dunc's, at the top of Woodseats Road. The shop was officially named Duncan's, but as the proprietor also doubled as the local pawnbroker, it was always affectionately known as Uncle Dunc's. These wonderful slippers were bought for the exorbitant price of two shillings and eleven pence, which prompted Mum to remark that she didn't know what the world was coming to, and that she should have had the sense to put the extra to, so as to buy me some good, hard-wearing shoes instead.

Actually, the year of 1944 was to bring the world a little nearer to the promise of 'Peace in our time,' made by Neville Chamberlain on his return from Munich in 1937, when he waved his bit of paper above his head. Except that the timing was a few years out.

In the Far Fast, the Burma Campaign was still being fought tenaciously and almost un-noticed in the Western world (the Allied soldiers had christened themselves 'the forgotten Army'), in the South West Pacific the whole area, including New Guinea, the Philippines, Malaya, the Solomon's and French Indo-China, had been secured by the Allies by the middle of 1944. In the Italian Campaign, fierce fighting was taking place and by May 25th the race for Rome was on.

But it was in Britain that history was being made in those first months of 1944. Preparations were taking place for the greatest armada in history, to set sail from England's south coast ports for landings on the continent of Europe. This then, in reply to Mum's remark, was what the world was coming to in the summer of 1944.

In January 1944, after a year of careful preparation, the Red Army began the push towards the successful liberation of the city of Leningrad, and the end of the 900 days-long siege.

In the Spring of 1944, in fashion-starved Britain, the Jigger coat had arrived. This was a three-quarter length jacket, and every girl who had enough clothing coupons was wearing one. Margaret, who of course was working by this time, had a friend who knew a little woman who could make these jackets from the plaid blankets which could be purchased, coupon-free, from the Sheffield Market. It all sounded a bit implausible to me, but Margaret managed to buy one of these much sought-after blankets, and had it made up by the lady in question. It was a huge success. It really was a splendid looking coat, and I would defy anyone, even today, to tell the difference between that jacket and one bought from a store.

It was truly amazing how the young women and girls at the time managed to look so smart when they could purchase so little. The year before, it was the Red and Black look, when almost all the young women were wearing red jackets and black skirts.

On Sunday afternoons, Brenda and I would make the occasional, very boring tram journey from the top of Smithywood Road to Firvale Hospital to visit Grandma Wilson. We always sat in the upstairs front bay of the tram, because we could see more of what was going on from this vantage point. Being very observant, and having a great interest in what the fashions were at any given time, we couldn't help but notice the increasing incidence of red and black, which the younger ladies were wearing on their Sunday afternoon strolls. We often made the journey more interesting by counting these apparitions, and as time went by, even we were surprised by the increasing numbers.

We spent a lot of our time riding on trams, did Brenda and I. We would often make the journey up to Meadowhead and back, just for the fun of flicking the seats over for the return trip, when the tram turned round at the terminus. The actual manoeuvre involved in turning it round never failed to impress us greatly. The Conductor would remove the cumbersome long pole from the underside of the tram, where it was always kept, and lift the trolley wheel from the 'going up wire' to the 'going down wire' as we called them. It was a spectacle of which we never tired.

Brenda's Dad was a tram-driver, and if he was actually driving a tram on which we were passengers, it definitely made our day. Being an employee meant that members of his family could enjoy all the facilities available at the Tramway Field, which was situated at Four Lane Ends – it's still there – and although there weren't many facilities to suit our age group, there was a very large see-saw some way past the pavilion. We spent many happy hours on that see-saw, sometimes the whole of the afternoon, taking a picnic and having a wonderful time, just sailing up and down on it.

I often look back to those lovely summer days during the war, when we were able to roam about at will, with never a thought of danger or fear of anyone. We didn't take a lot of amusing as children, we were quite happy to amuse ourselves. There wasn't much in the way of toys, and bicycles were only for the rich kids, not for the likes of us. It was no earthly use pining for one, because there was no money to spare for such things, and we knew it. I learned at a very early age that it was no use crying for the moon, because there was no way that it could be obtained. We were provided with everything which Mum and Dad could afford when we were growing up and, in the main, we were quite happy with our lot.

Sometimes, when Hilda was at a loose end, Mum made us take her along with us. This didn't happen very often, because she was rarely short of something to do, or someone to do it with, but very occasionally it did. I loved her dearly most of the time, but when we had to take her with us she seemed to grow horns. Her favourite saying at these times was, 'I'll tell Mum'. No matter what we wished to do, she wanted to do something else.

On one of these outings, we were going on a picnic, up around Beauchief Abbey. Hilda was about seven at the time, and she had eaten her sandwiches before we had reached the end of Archer Road. She really could be the most aggravating child sometimes, and when we were about half-way there, she climbed up a tree and flatly refused to come down. No amount of cajolery or threats would get her out of that tree, and in the end we just left her there, and continued on our way with 'I'll tell my Mum' ringing in our ears. We never gave her another thought, spent the afternoon by the Abbey and round the Golf Course, and wended our way home just after tea.

I was greeted by a very angry Mother, and a very smug looking Hilda, who had wandered home in her own time and without mishap at about 4 o'clock. I got the hiding of my life that day, but it was not completely unexpected. As I was reminded very forcefully by my Mother, leaving one's little sister to fend for herself, even if she was sitting up a tree, wasn't the kindest thing in the world to do. Later, as I lay in my bed, smarting from the slapped legs and the injustice of it all, I realised that even if it wasn't one of the kindest things that I had ever done, it was certainly one of the most satisfying.

She was a strange child, was Hilda. One of her most endearing qualities was her love of stray cats. If she ever found one of these animals wandering around in the street, whether it was lost (and they seldom were) or not, she would pick it up, and push it gently down our cellar grate. Many was the time Mum would open the cellar door, to be greeted by a cat or two walking through into the living room.

I'll say one thing. With Hilda around, there was never a dull moment.

. . . leave school at fourteen

THE BEGINNING OF JUNE 1944 was very cloudy and wet, and as we awoke on the 6th, although it had improved a little, it still wasn't an ideal summer's day. This was the moment that the whole country had been waiting for, for many a long year, when the news came over the radio that the Allies were landing on the beaches in Normandy. The armada had sailed, and the invasion was on.

It had originally been intended to take place on the 4th – the day that the Americans entered Rome – but the weather in the Channel was bad, and after having waited with the ships ready and the troops and equipment on board for days, it had to be the 6th, or the whole operation would have to be cancelled. Fortunately, there was a slight improvement in the weather conditions, and by breakfast-time everyone in the country was informed about the landings. It was the longest day in our lives.

The landings took place on five Normandy beaches, which covered a stretch of coastline nearly fifty miles long, between the Dunes of Varreville, and Ouistreham. They were code-named *Utah, Omaha, Gold, Juno* and *Sword*, names which can still be recited by almost anyone who can remember D-Day 1944.

Hitler was sleeping at the time, and his aides at first didn't wish to disturb him. It was a well-known fact in Hitler's inner circle that when he flew into a rage, his anger was so great that he had been known to chew on the carpets. Maybe he was always in a bad mood first thing in the morning and they preferred not to be on the receiving end on this particular day, or perhaps they underestimated the importance of the unfolding events on the Normandy beaches. For whatever reason, it turned out to be a grave mistake, for when their esteemed leader awoke from his slumbers, it was already far too late.

Many accounts of these landings have been written. Suffice it to say that by the end of the first 24 hours, a foothold had been gained on the European mainland. The cost in men, estimated at 2,500, was nothing short of a miracle when compared with the first day of the Battle of the Somme in 1916, when 20,000 men perished.

As the early summer of 1944 rolled on, my future was coming under the spotlight at home. It wasn't so much being discussed, as sorted out. There was never much likelihood of further education. Working-class girls were catered for, and looked after, fed and clothed, until the time came when they could 'earn their keep'. This, in my case was at fourteen years of age, or at fifteen, when the School Certificate could be taken in the last year of schooling. The School Certificate, if obtained in the final examination, could lead to a college education, but this was never an option, because those were the days when College grants were unheard of and parents were expected to finance their children for a further three years, or however long it took to get them through College or University.

Art College was where I would have liked to have gone, but as Mum pointed out, what use would that be when the time came for getting a job? Girls didn't need to go to College, anyhow, for by the time they reached their early twenties they were usually married with families, and all the sacrifices that parents were expected to make had then been a waste of time. No, the rules were, leave school at fourteen and get a job like everyone else did. So that was that sorted out.

Margaret was already working, and had tried one or two different jobs during the past three years, but now she was nicely settled in the Sheffield Telephone Exchange. This, according to Mum, was a feather in anyone's cap, getting a Government job. She was a great believer, having seen unemployment and the miseries it could bring, in 'getting under the big umbrella', which was how she always referred to the Civil Service. It was decided that I would write and apply to join Margaret under the same umbrella.

I cannot remember being bothered either way whilst my entire future was being arranged in this cavalier fashion, but I knew the rules, and I was quite happy at that time to abide by them. It was only in the years following that I wished that there had been some other options considered. At thirteen years old, I was too young to have many ideas of my own. That came later, by which time, it was much too late.

And so I applied to the GPO, which was situated in Fitzalan Square, and was granted an interview, which was conducted in a part of the telephone exchange, as yet only half built, known by scores of operators in later years as 'Joint Trunk'. There was a hearing test, and a small examination to prove that the interviewee was not illiterate, and a voice test, which took place in the Exchange amongst all the operators, who were going about their daily work, as usual. I remember thinking, as I walked into the very busy room, that it sounded like an extremely bad day in a parrot house. There seemed to be hundreds of girls in there, all talking at the same time, with plugs clanging and clicking, and bells ringing all over the place. All in all, my first foray into the Sheffield Exchange was quite a sobering experience, and one which remains with me to this day.

I received a letter a few days later, and was informed that I had been accepted and would be sent for as soon as a vacancy arose after leaving school the following Easter, 1945. Mother then had to inform the school, and the Headmaster was horrified. The school reports after the Summer examinations were just about to go out, and Mr Kay requested that my parents came up to the school to see him.

I was mystified by this unusual happening, but gave Mum his letter when I got home from school. Dad couldn't have the time off work, but Mum duly made the not-inconsiderable journey to the school to see the Headmaster. I never knew the full details of what took place between the two of them that day, I only know that I left school the following Easter as planned, and started work under the 'big umbrella' the following June. However, I still have my school report from 1944 and I seem to have done quite well in the Summer exams.

I realised that Mr Kay wanted me to stay on at school for the fourth year, but I can't say that at the time I was particularly interested either way. In view of what happened a few days later, he was probably glad

Save fuel

COAL · COKE · ELECTRICITY
GAS · FUEL OIL · PARAFFIN

for the factories

Have a fire in one room only. Breakfast in the kitchen and save lighting the sitting-room fire until you really have to.

Issued by the
Mines Department

to see the back of me.

We had at school a lovely lady who taught Art and Needlework. The Art bit was great, but my needlework always did leave a lot to be desired. She was very tall and very thin, wore her hair in a bun, and always perched on the end of her nose were a pair of small rimless spectacles. She was, in fact, everone's typical picture of a Schoolmarm, and to complete the picture she had the thinnest pair of legs ever to be seen outside a canary cage. We called her 'Sparrowlegs'. In class one day, she was somewhere at the back of the room, and reaching over the adjacent desk to retrieve a pair of scissors from the floor, I inadvertently stuck my leg out in the aisle, just as the aforementioned teacher was passing down, on her way towards the front of the class.

Needless to say, she went flying over my outstretched leg, falling in a heap onto the floor, and knocking herself unconscious on the corner of the desk in front as she went down. It took four pupils and the Geography master, who on hearing the commotion from the classroom next door had rushed in to render assistance, to extricate her from the tangle in the aisle. By the time she was placed gently on the floor with a cushion under her head, a couple more teachers appeared from somewhere, and she was tenderly carried out of the room and down the stairs to the Staff room. It was a complete accident, and after the facts were sifted through nothing more was ever said about it, but the lady was away from school for quite a long time, and Art lessons were never the same for the remainder of my time at school.

The most comical aspect of the whole sorry affair was the fact that the Geography master was the smallest teacher in the school, and whilst the rescue was taking place the remainder of the class were having silent hysterics watching his valiant efforts. It was a good thing he didn't catch anyone laughing. He may have been the smallest, but he was also the teacher with the worst temper, a virtual dab-hand at flinging the blackboard rubber across the classroom when he got his dander up.

Whilst I was endeavouring to reduce the pupil-teacher ratio at school, one or two German Generals were trying to do the same to Adolf Hitler, and to replace him with someone who would start peace negotiations with the Allies. But the attempt sadly failed; four men lost their lives in the explosion but Hitler was still alive

The war continued, and so did everything else. There was always a stony silence in the house when the news bulletins were being read out. It was an unwritten law that everyone kept quiet, in case any vital snippet of news was missed. We only had one paper delivered to the house and that was the *Daily Worker*. I never read it myself, finding it extremely boring. In any case, Brenda and I got all the information that we wanted from the Newsreels at the cinema.

There were five cinemas within walking distance from home, the *Abbeydale*, the *Heeley Palace*, *Heeley Coliseum*, *Chantrey* and *Woodseats* Picture Palaces, and there was usually a different film showing at each one on any given day. We spent most of the money which we could scrape together at the pictures. Sometimes we managed to afford the stalls, but mostly we sat in the very front seats – known as the pit (or more often called the flea-pit). It mattered not a jot to either of us where we sat because we always enjoyed ourselves. It was only the First House, of course, because we always had to be home early. During the wintertime it was usually the Matinées we went to, because of the blackout. We didn't know what it was like to be able to walk around at night and to be able to see where we were going.

Anything and everything which could be seen from the air was either switched off or covered up in such a way that they were less than useless. We never went anywhere without a torch, but even they only had a mere pinhole of illumination to light up the ground, (it was not permitted to shine torches skywards even to find the yale lock.)

Trams wended their way through the darkened streets like clattering wraithes in the night, showing barely enough light inside them to distinguish the seats, and buses, ambulances and all other vehicles had their headlights shuttered to show just a glimmer of light. Street lights showed no light at all, and it was the easiest thing in the world to walk into a lamp post, I did it myself more than once. Chip shops were simple to locate; we only had to follow our noses.

Many ingenious ways were found in many homes to extinguish the house lights when the outside door was opened, and it was quite common to find, on entering someone's home, extra wires leading from the door and going in all directions, which hazardous practice often presented as much danger inside as there was out.

But we got used to it and much humour was found in the situation. I remember one winter's night particularly well, when the door opened and Mr Pashley walked in. He lived in the corresponding house to ours in the yard below. He looked around in a bemused fashion, saw Mum, and said, 'Ee, I'm sorry, love, I've walked up the wrong bloody passage!' Things like that were always happening, but they were the things which made life worthwhile and which we could laugh about.

A *death, and a birth*

A S THE SUMMER OF 1944 WORE ON, the Allies were making great headway across the continent of Europe. After the first confusing days, when the British and Americans were trying to break out of the beach areas, and the enemy were trying desperately to stop them, the Allies started to move forward. On August 25th General Charles De Gaulle walked into Paris and the French capital was free of the German conquerors once again.

In Eastern Europe, the Russians were pushing the Germans back towards the west, and by the end of August 1944 they had cleared all their own territory of the invader.

September 17th 1944 is a date which I remember well, though perhaps best known as the historic day when Operation Market Garden was launched by the Allies and the British First Airborne Division landed near Arnhem, in the Netherlands. But it was also the day when two other events happened which more directly affected me at the time. Air raids, which much of the population suffered during the first years of the War, were no longer a threat, the Luftwaffe having been denied access to our skies by repeated bombing raids. But Hitler's secret weapon, the V1 pilotless plane, was still making life difficult and extremely dangerous for the citizens of London and the South, although here in the North we were not much affected by them. I believe we had just one over Sheffield, but it passed over and harmlessly exploded on the moors, nearer to Manchester.

The V1s were known as 'Buzz Bombs' by people in Southern England, who had to live with their constant noise on a daily basis. They sounded like the engine of a two-stroke motor bike as they winged across overhead, but when the engine note ceased, it was time to duck and take cover, for it meant that the bomb was on its way down to earth, and the imminent explosion wouldn't be far behind.

The newer V2, which was to arrive over the country in late September, was a rocket, and gave no warning of the impending explosion. Both these weapons were visited on the South in their hundreds and caused much misery and loss of life to many families.

As there were no pilots in these monstrosities, it was figured that there was no-one to care, either one way or the other, whether lights were visible from the air or not, so the decision was made to lift the blackout restrictions which had been part of our lives since 1939. Sunday 17th September was the night chosen to put the new regulations into effect. After that date there would be no more shouts from irate wardens to 'Put that light out', often accompanied by an expletive or two depending on the severity of the misdemeanour, and we all felt that it was the end of an era. That Sunday was the end of an era for our family, for it was also the day that Grandma Wilson died in her sixty-fourth year, in Firvale Infirmary, at the other side of the city.

Grandma Wilson, christened Alice Ellen Taylor, was born in Sheffield on 31st December 1881. She was brought up on a farm in Heeley, a strange place in these modern times, one would think for a farm to be, but nevertheless my Great Grandparents and their family had a farm, somewhere around the back of where Ponsford's furniture shop now stands, on Heeley Bottom.

In 1900, she met and married my Grandfather, George Wall, and they had four children; my mother, Gladys, born in 1902; Alice, born in 1904; Emily in 1906 and George Junior in 1910. Grandfather Wall came originally from Ashford-in-the Water, in Derbyshire, and he walked all the way to Sheffield to look for work in the late 1890s. He laboured for a time on the building of Sheffield Town Hall, and then he obtained work when the tram track was being laid to Millhouses. Eventually he became a coachman for Proctor's the drapers on Pinstone Street, and when my Mother was about three years old he was promoted to Head Coachman, and they moved into the house in Monmouth Street, with stables, which went with the job. My Mother had a very happy childhood when the family lived in that house, and she spoke many times of her love for the horses which were stabled there when we were children. But in 1913, when she was eleven years old, her much-loved father contracted pneumonia, and within a few days he was dead.

He was just thirty-five years old when this tragedy occurred, and Grandma was left a widow at thirty-two, with four children to care for. They had to leave the house, which left them virtually on the streets. There was no widow's pension in those good old days, which we hear so much about, and the family had to move in with Great Grandma for a while.

The farm had been sold by this time, and Great Grandma lived with her two sons in Artisan Place, which was just off Wellhead Road, at Heeley. Using the money which had been left over from the insurance, Grandma opened a small house-windowed shop in Gleadless Road, where she sold tripe and all the other things which were sold in tripe shops in those days. Neither Grandma nor her children had an easy life, from then onwards, but they survived, and in 1916 she married Grandpa Wilson. When he returned from the War, they settled down in one of the three houses which Great Grandma had bought in Artisan Place, from the proceeds of the sale of the farm,

She gave birth to another baby, when my mother was nineteen, but she was stillborn, and after that she was never really fit and well again. When I was born, she was only fifty years old, but I always remember her even when I was very small, as being a very old lady. She suffered from Paget's disease, and although she was quite tall, when she was younger I can only remember her being a very tiny, hump-backed lady, very badly deformed, and hardly able to walk about.

On September 17th 1944, she died, and although she was only sixty-three years old, she looked at least twenty years older, a very old lady who had lived through two World Wars and much personal tragedy. She had great faith, and I knew even at thirteen years old that she wasn't sorry to leave her suffering behind, and go to join her maker.

But earlier that year there had been happier news in our family, for in March 1944, Joyce was married, in the church by the side of

Portchester Castle in Fareham, near Portsmouth. It was not possible for any of the family to go down from Sheffield for the wedding, but there was much excitement about the event, and a wedding present was duly dispatched. In the following July, on our return from school, we found much to-ing and fro-ing taking place between our house and Aunt Alice's, next door. A telegram had arrived from Portsmouth to say that Joyce and her new husband Ernest, who was on a weeks leave from the Navy, would be arriving the next day for a visit. The to-ing and fro-ing was due to the fact that beds in our house were at a premium, and in Aunty's there was a spare bedroom. (This arrangement came in very handy over the years, for a variety of occasions.)

I rushed home from school the next day, and for the first time was introduced to Ern. He was, and still is, a lovely man. But in those days, he had the unusual trait of getting along famously with children. He loved them. He took Hilda and I into town one morning to get some strawberries for Mum and Dad's anniversary tea, which they were to celebrate on July 11th and which, coinciding with their visit, was going to be a special family occasion. As I recall, the most special part of the day was entering a Milk Bar for the first time in my short life, and partaking of the various delights on offer in Marsden's on Cambridge Street. I felt like a princess, and the experience – almost every minute of it – has stuck firmly in my mind ever since.

In complete contrast, the celebration tea has faded away in the mists of time. It must have been a very extra special tea, with the strawberries and all, but I remember nothing about it.

Joyce's elder daughter was born the following December, on the eve of Ern's departure from Portsmouth to Trincomalee Harbour in what we then called Ceylon (now Sri Lanka). On the day after she was born he was due to sail early in the day, but was given special leave to visit the hospital in Southampton to have a look at his new daughter, then he had to catch the train to Rosyth, in Scotland, where he joined his ship the same evening. She was three years old before he saw her again. They were hard times indeed for young couples.

He sent Mum some tea from Ceylon whilst he was stationed there, a Godsend to a family which – in normal times – drank enough tea to float the *Queen Mary*. In the same parcel was a letter to Hilda and I, which in spite of all the other people he must have been expected to write to, being all those miles away from his home and his family, he had taken the trouble to write. With it was a a box of Spangles packed in a mini wooden crate. Thinking about it, I suppose paper was in short supply too, like most other things at that time, for it was the first time that we had ever received a parcel in a wooden box. Those delicious boiled streets became quite commonplace after the end of the war, but were unknown to us at the time. All in all, Joyce's new husband was a great hit in our family, especially the younger end. For myself, I have never lost the fondness that I felt then for this very special young man, who was so kind to two young children who were complete strangers to him until his visit to Sheffield in 1944.

Always a bit of a mystery

O NE EVENING recently a man was being interviewed on television, and I heard him advise: 'If you ever meet a man who tells you he was at Arnhem in 1944, shake him by the hand and buy him a drink'. I remember well the news coming out of Arnhem during this time. It was mostly bad and it was the one episode of the war which held my interest the whole time. I was getting older, and my understanding was much more acute than during the early years. Each morning I said heartfelt prayers for the men at Arnhem, and in school every day we repeated them before lessons began. When the full story was known we were all completely devastated to think that men could go through all that pain and suffering only to be deprived of victory in the end.

There has always been doubt about the wisdom of Montgomery's plan, which he believed would see the War finished before the end of 1944. The plan was to parachute and land by glider large numbers of men behind the German lines to seize bridges across the rivers Maas and the Waal, which were vital for the Allies' continued advance into Germany. It all went wrong, and at what cost. Of the 10,000 men of the Arnhem force, less than 2,500 reached safety. Figures for the Dutch civilians caught up in the area during this times and in the dreadful winter of privation which followed have never been verified, but could have been as high as 10,000. Montgomery, however, always insisted that Arnhem been 90 percent successful

It brought to my mind a phrase quoted after the Battle of the Somme in 1916, when the troops were likened to 'Lions led by donkeys'. I can't say that I have ever fully subscribed to that remark, but one cannot help noticing that the donkeys in question – or rather the ones in overall charge – are usually sitting somewhere comfortable well away from where the lions are being led. Prince Bernhard of the Netherlands was quoted as saying, 'My country can never again afford the luxury of another Montgomery success'.

As all this was taking place on the Continent of Europe, Grandma was laid to rest in Ecclesall churchyard. The day before, Mum and Aunty Alice needed to go into town, and Grandma was by then 'lying in state' in the front room at Artisan Place. Although she had died in the hospital, and had been laid out by the undertakers, it was customary to bring the coffin home on the day before the funeral and overnight, for relatives and friends to call and pay their respects, and someone was required to watch over her for a couple of hours. As Grandpa was at work and nobody else was available for this rather gruesome task, being the eldest grandchild at liberty I was nominated. I remember it well, sitting in that room for what seemed like hours, as far away from the trestle and its burden as was humanly possible, and wishing fervently that the ground would open and swallow me up.

Mum's parting words had been, 'Now, there's nothing to be afraid of. She would never have harmed you when she was alive, and she certainly won't harm you now'. I knew all that, of course, but it didn't alter the fact that it was a daunting task for any thirteen-year-old girl, and I have never forgotten that Thursday afternoon. It was a very warm and sunny day and the window had to be kept open, and it was my job to make sure that no cats got into the room. As far as I knew there were no cats within miles of Grandma's front room, but I did my utmost to be very diligent, and I know that my eyes rarely left that window for the whole of the time that I was there.

The funeral progressed without incident, and the boiled ham and tongue tea – which was obligatory on such occasions, and which had been provided from the meagre rations of the whole family – was held in Grandma's house in Artisan Place and was fairly civilised. There was nothing for anyone to fight about, for Grandma had few, if any worldly goods. Not many people had, in those days, which at least, made things much simpler for the people left behind.

Uncle George's wife, Aunty Phyllis, was by nature a very jolly lady, and she made a joke about something or other to me, which made us both laugh. Mother frowned greatly at this, and afterwards I heard her say to Dad that she would never forgive Phyllis for making a 'Pippy Show' of her mother's funeral. I half expected to be hauled over the coals myself, for daring to laugh at such a time, but she never mentioned it, and of course she forgave Aunty Phyllis. The next time they met they were the best of friends.

Grandpa Wilson was used to fending for himself, and he never asked for any help. Once or twice, I went straight from school to clean the steps and window sills, and do the things which didn't take much skill and knowhow. I always liked Grandpa, but I could never understand my mother's attitude towards him, because when she spoke of her teenage years it always seemed to me that he was very good to her. She told me that once during the First World War, he met her from her work when he was home on leave, and because it was raining and she had holes in her shoes, her took her shopping, and bought her a brand new pair. Brand new shoes were not normal in those days, and she told me how proud she felt to be wearing them. I know that when we were tiny, he pushed us all over the place in our prams and pushchairs when he was out of work in the 1930s, but it seemed that he could never do anything quite right for his grownup stepchildren. He always appeared to be a solemn, very taciturn old man, but I believe that he was fond of us in his own way, and I was certainly fond of him.

He told me many stories about his army service, in India and in other places. It was Grandpa who put me off curry for life, with the dire warning, 'Never eat curry, lass, unless you know who prepared it'. He told me that when he was stationed in India, no British soldier ever ate a curry, unless he had cooked it himself, because the flavour disguised all sorts of peculiar things, which may or may not be in the pot. If there was rotten meat there, it couldn't be detected if it was curried.

He was in the trenches at the Battle of Mons in August 1916, and he was one of the many British and French soldiers who saw the Angel of Mons. This, according to Grandpa, was an apparition which appeared in the night sky over the trenches in the shape of a beautiful, angelic lady. Apparently, she was bathed in a heavenly light, and had wings, which shimmered in the darkness. I was never quite sure why she appeared, I only know that Grandpa was adamant that, along with hundreds of other soldiers, he had witnessed it. Whatever else the Angel was, she couldn't have been the herald of a great victory, because the British and the French Army had to fall back to the Marne River, but Grandpa said that when she appeared, everyone felt greatly comforted.

He was always a bit of a mystery. He just appeared in the lives of Grandma and her four children one day, and apart from his service in the army they never found out much about his previous life. The only thing he ever told them was that when he was sixteen he had a fight with his father, hit him with a pitchfork, then ran away and joined the army. Where all this drama took place, no-one ever knew, but he certainly wasn't a Yorkshire man, because his accent wasn't quite right.

Mother was convinced that he'd 'done his father in' with the pitchfork, but I always thought this explanation a little fanciful. When, some years later, an official called to see him about his state pension, Grandpa sent him packing with a king-sized flea in his ear, and as far as I know, up until the day he died at a well-turned seventy-years-old, he never received a pension. Of course, the whole affair could have been much more simple than murder or mayhem. He may have had another wife tucked away somewhere in his murky past. This was never even contemplated by the family. We were far too respectable to have a bigamist in the ranks, but as my husband is delighted to tell anyone, Grandma's younger brother was no paragon.

He spent his share of the money from the sale of the family farm, then became a tramp, and spent the rest of his days on the open road, only turning up in Sheffield for his Christmas dinner. He breathed his last under a hedge in Dorset when I was three years old, and Grandma didn't hear about it until his tramping companion, a very disreputable looking man with a ginger beard, knocked on her door and gave her a sixpenny piece, which was all that Jim (or Ratapan, as Grandma always called him) had in the world when he died. His friend was entrusted to take it to his sister, if he happened to be passing through Sheffield. A poignant tale, which helps a lot to restore one's faith in human nature.

A childhood put on hold

A S THE LAST CHRISTMAS of the war approached, everyone seemed highly delighted by the way things were progressing. The Allies were closing in on Germany on all fronts, and it was only a matter of time before it would all be over and the lads would be coming home. We didn't give a great deal of thought to what would happen when the fighting stopped and the politicians took over, but that is another story.

By this time the pre-Christmas festivities were getting under way at school. There was very little evidence of anything very exciting in the food line for our yearly form party, but most hard-pressed mothers managed to send their offspring to school with something or other.

That particular Christmas, I managed to coax a jelly out of mum. It was probably a home-concocted one, which mum was quite good at, because jellies for some reason were very hard to come by, during that time. I don't know why, fresh fruit was always quite plentiful during the summer months, except of course, the ones which were obviously imported, like oranges and bananas. I tasted my very first banana, when the War ended, and I thought they were awful. Oranges, when available, were rationed to children under five and pregnant mothers, and as I didn't come under either of these categories, they were a complete mystery to me for years.

Although I set off for school proudly carrying my jelly in Mum's glass fruit-bowl, unfortunately it never reached the school party, because it slipped out of my hands as I was crossing Meersbrook Park. This was the second dish that I had broken in a week, and I was not the flavour of the month on my return from school.

The previous week I had 'gone over the bridge' with a basin (in our neighbourhood, to go shopping on Abbeydale Road was always referred to as 'going over the bridge' because the railway bridge at the bottom of Woodseats Road had to be crossed before reaching the shops), to fetch some pork dripping. I made the journey on my roller-skate – I say skate because for some reason, I only had one. Mr Chatterton, the Pork Butcher, had sold out of his very popular dripping, and on the return journey, I dropped the basin and smashed it. Mum didn't believe me when I related the circumstances of the abortive trip to the shops. She insisted that I had broken the basin before I went into the Pork Butcher's, and she immediately confiscated my roller-skate for ever, and tossed it into the dustbin.

This was one of the many times during my childhood when I felt very hard done by, and which convinced me, even more, that I had either been adopted from a Foundling Home, or had been left on the doorstep in a cardboard box by a passing band of gypsies. I had, even then, a very colourful imagination.

Actually I was very fortunate to be allowed to attend the Christmas party at all. Looking back to my last year at school, it seemed that I was developing a tendency towards becoming accident-prone. A week or two before, a friend and I had been on library duty during the lunch hour. The library was situated on the landing, outside the Headmaster's study.

It was not a very grand affair, merely a selection of books in four or five book-cases, but it was the only one we had, and the school in general was very proud of it. Books would be borrowed, signed out, and returned within the week, and on this particular day it was our turn on the much-sought-after rota. When things were quiet, which they often were, we amused ourselves in a variety of ways, and one of my favourites was to swing from the landing above. It was possible to do this by climbing up three or four steps from the library, turning round and launching oneself into space, grasping hold of the floor above in mid-flight. My friend, being much smaller than I, was unable to participate in this enjoyable pastime, as she couldn't reach the landing above, no matter how hard she tried. So, not to be outdone, as I was merrily swinging away, she climbed a few more steps, and from behind she leapt on to my back, thus causing us both to fall backwards onto the concrete steps below.

Naturally, she fell beneath me, and so cushioned my fall, but she was out cold, having cracked her head very hard as we fell. She was taken by ambulance to the hospital and kept in overnight for observation, but luckily not a lot of harm had been done, although she was away from school for a couple of weeks.

The Headmaster, a very fair man, as mentioned earlier, reserved judgement on the whole sorry affair until she returned to school, and the whole episode was put down to a childish prank that went wrong, and which could have been a lot worse. The only punishment received was a very strong ticking off, and banishment from the library landing for the pair of us, for ever.

For its time, I suppose, the school which I attended was quite a progressive one. School societies were an integral part of the curriculum, and were very popular with pupils and teachers alike. On joining the school in the first year, all pupils were given the option on which of the Societies to join. There was music, Arts and Crafts, sports and a variety of others, including Drama. My preference was for the Musical Society, and it was during these weekly sessions that I began to appreciate music of all kinds. We had frequent visits to the City Hall for the afternoon concerts given by the Hallé Orchestra, and these outings were highlights in our school lives.

The Hallé conductor at the time was John Barbirolli, who having succeeded the great Arturo Toscanini in 1937 as conductor of the New York Philharmonic Orchestra, had been appointed to the Hallé Orchestra in 1943. The Leader was Jean Punier, one of the most handsome men I had ever seen. He was tall, blonde-haired and extremely dashing, and he quickly became second only to Errol Flynn in my affections. I was grateful for many things in my school life, but the privilege of seeing these two masters of their profession in the Hallé Orchestra was an experience which I still remember vividly as one of the better things in my life.

At Christmastide the Dramatic and Musical Societies were in the forefront of any entertainment performed for the delight, or otherwise, of the assembled school, and in 1944 two particular boys stand out in my memory. One of them played the violin – very badly. He obviously hadn't been taking lessons for very long, and for all I know, in later life he may well have become a virtuoso. I'll say one thing in his favour; he was a trier. He could produce notes from that violin never previously heard outside a cattery, and he tortured both the instrument and his long-suffering captive audience with almost demonic pleasure. We were much too polite to laugh, and much too afraid of the wrath of the teachers, but we cringed at every tortuous note and applauded wildly when he ceased his recital, hoping fervently that he wouldn't treat us to an encore.

The other boy was the star of the Dramatic Society, and this particular year he performed two solo, one-act plays. His name as I remember was Green, and if any lad was born to tread the boards it was he. One of his plays was *The Monkey's Paw*, and the other was *Sweeney Todd the Demon Barber of Fleet Street*, both of which were highly entertaining and extremely well done. I never heard of him again after I left school, but I have never forgotten the talent which showed through even then and often wondered what became of him in later lifer. I don't suppose it ever occurred to him to consider acting as a career. He probably took up banking, or possibly politics would have been more in his line.

Just as Christmas was almost upon us, the Germans began their last big offensive of the War, in the Ardennes – the Battle of the Bulge – Hitler's last desperate attempt to halt the advance of the Allies. It failed, after a month's bitter fighting, and by January 1945 the Allied advance continued.

Sometimes, when I look back to those far off days, it seems to me that somehow my childhood was put on hold for a while, in limbo, as it were. Imagine a childhood without ice-cream, for example. To be sure, a man would come round the streets periodically on his Wall's tricycle, with the 'Stop me and buy one ' slogan written on the front, but he didn't actually sell ice-cream, only the fruity water ices in their three-cornered cardboard containers. We just had to poke a finger in at the bottom and push the concoction out at the top, a very absorbing pastime. Maybe, if we had been taught the basics of cookery when at school, I would have become a Cordon Bleu chef, or maybe, if sweets hadn't been rationed for most of the war and beyond, I wouldn't still have most of my own teeth. Interesting observations, but I shall never know, and it's too late to worry about such mundane things now.

When rung today, church bells welcome one to worship, or joyously to a wedding, but in those days it was against the law for the bells to ring, because that was to be the signal for an invasion. There was no Bonfire Night or fireworks for the duration of the war, and the childhood thrill of being allowed to stay up a little later, and sit on a seat in the back field in front of a blazing fire, watching the scores of coloured explosions of lights in the night sky, had to wait until the war ended. By that time, of course, I no longer considered myself a child. We grew up very quickly in those days; going out to work at fourteen and having the responsibility of a job made very sure of that. A friend told me recently, that the day after his fourteenth birthday, he started work down the pit, and after being taken to his work station he was left, on his own, in charge of some equipment for the whole of his shift. Apart from his miner's lamp, he was in total darkness, with only the rodents for company, and he admitted that he was petrified. He stayed there until his fellow miners collected him, on their return from the coal face and took him up top. We laughed with him, as he related his story, but I wouldn't like to think that any fourteen-year old of my acquaintance would have to go through an experience like that today.

As 1945 was getting under way, we were beginning to understand just what Hitler's New Order really meant. Information was emerging, as the Allies moved into the German heartland, about the concentration camps which were scattered across the occupied territories, and in Germany itself. A horrified world heard for the first time the names which have gone down in the pages of history, to the everlasting shame of the German nation. Auschwitz-Birkenau, Treblinka, Chelmo, Bergen-Belsen, Ravensbruch, Buchenwald, Dachau and others, in which six million Jews were exterminated, and thousands of others, of all races were systematically worked to death as slave labourers. Those years between 1939 and 1945 should never be forgotten, for the magnitude of man's inhumanity against man.

In the Pacific, by the beginning of 1945, the Americans were regaining the ground lost in the aftermath of Pearl Harbour. The island of Iwo Jima was crucial if the Allies were to be able to even contemplate an invasion of the Japanese mainland, and the battle for the island, which began in February, became the bloodiest and costliest in the history of the American marines. By mid-March the island was secured, thus enabling the first bombing raid on the Japanese mainland in April 1945.

Victory in Burma, came, also, for the jungle fighters of the British and Commonwealth armies, and when it came it was decisive. The Japanese, despite their plimsolls end cardboard tanks, had fought tenaciously every inch of the way, but had been out-thought, out-witted and out-fought by an equally tenacious foe, and a very cunning General, William Slim.

We were not sure how the war was going to end, nor were we sure when, but as Easter approached the mood on the home front was jubilant, because everyone was certain that it would come sooner rather than later. There were at least two members of the family who were feeling the strain a little more than the rest of us, and who would be breathing a sigh of relief when things got back to normal. Aunty Alice and Uncle Ted both worked at Laycock's, on munitions work. When the War was in its infancy, it was decreed (and there were many decrees about one thing or another at that time) that all able married women, between certain ages, and who had no family ties – such as young children or elderly dependants – must find work, to help in the War effort. As Uncle Ted was already working at Laycock's, and the factory was quite near, Aunty Alice got a job early on in the War. They both worked shifts, but were very rarely on the same one, thus making their home life extremely hazardous. They barely saw each other some weeks, except to nod 'Good morning' or 'Good evening' as they were passing through, on their way to or from work, but they both took it in good part, and like the rest of us managed to survive. Most of the family were blessed with a fairly exceptional sense of humour, and over the years it has stood us in good stead.

Another decree was to have only five inches of water in the bath, and to share the bath water, when possible. I don't know how the makers of these decrees were brought up, but it certainly wasn't the same way that we were raised. We had been sharing the bath-water for years. When every drop of water has to be heated up in a gas copper in the kitchen, and transferred with a ladling can into the waiting tin bath, not a great deal of hot water is wasted. Bath night was quite a ritual in our house. It wasn't so bad when we were smaller, as bathing in front of all and sundry is no big deal for an infant, but as we were growing up we required a little more privacy. The promise made by Lloyd George after the First World War, of 'Homes fit for heroes to live in', which presumably meant having a proper bathroom, hadn't yet reached the ears of our landlord. On bath night, the copper was filled from the cold tap with the ladling can. This took quite a time, and was not one of the tasks over which we fought.

Then the zinc bath was carted up from the cellar. It wasn't particularly heavy, but was very cumbersome, and would clang against the walls on the way up, and Mum would be yelling above the din, 'Mind my walls, they'll not be fit to be seen'. If we'd had a delivery of coal during the week, the bath would usually have a film of coal dust over it, and by the time it reached the top of the cellar steps, having been manoeuvred round all the corners by two giggling, high-spirited children, we could have been quite easily mistaken for a couple of chimney sweeps. The bath then had to be cleaned, inside and out, before the kitchen door was firmly closed and the bathing could commence. The process of getting the water from the copper into the bath was also very time-consuming, and by the time the three of us had finished the whole procedure had taken about two hours. The bath was then emptied and the copper was refilled, ready for Mum and Dad to repeat the process when we were all in bed. We never had the luxury of taking a bath any time we wished; bath night was a fixture, and to quote the old saying, 'Every week we had a bath, whether we needed it or not'.

Just after I left school, it was broadcast from Washington that Francis Delano Roosevelt, the President of the United States, had died and that he was to be succeeded by the Vice-President, Harry S. Truman. Although we were not aware of it at the time, we were now moving into another of the Ages of Man. The Atomic Age was just around the corner, and Harry S. Truman could be said to be the man with starting gun. When he took office, he knew little or nothing about the 'Manhattan Project', the project designed to develop the first Atomic Bomb. During his first few months in office the nuclear bomb became the frightening reality, and the main reason for the Cold War, which was to remain with us for the next forty-five years.

I suppose it could be said, that relations between the Western Allies and the Soviet Union had never been warm, but we were all fighting the same enemy between 1939 and 1945 and everyone just got on with the job. But in August 1944 the uneasy friendship cooled a little, when the Red Army reached the outskirts of Warsaw. The Poles, knowing how near the Russians were to the city, rose up against their oppressors, expecting the Russians to help, but they didn't. The Red Army was ordered to stay on the banks of the River Vistula, and not to interfere with the Poles, who were fighting for their lives and their capital city. Despite pleas from the Polish Government in Exile, via the Western Allies, the Russians stayed where they mere, and the Polish partisans were crushed, and, as a horrified world looked on, Warsaw was razed to the ground. The fragile alliance which began in 1939 received a severe denting during that time, and never fully recovered from it.

Full of hope . . .

I LEFT SCHOOL AT EASTER, and waited impatiently at home, until the promised vacancy arose at the GPO. It was quite a long wait, for I didn't start my new job until June 2nd. Mum was a great believer in all the old adages, and the one about the devil finding work for idle hands was one of her favourites. Any illusions, on my part, of reading most of the books in Highfield Library, or generally lazing around for a week or two, were quickly shattered when Mum started the spring cleaning.

A new fashion in interior design had arrived in the neighbourhood with the coming of Spring and the general euphoria at the way the War was going. It was called graining. Mum had it on good authority from a lady living down the road, that it 'looked lovely, and was ever so easy to do'. Graining, as I remember, looked pretty average, and was very hard work. First of all a blowlamp had to be acquired from somewhere – Dad was sure there was one in the cellar, but it turned out that there wasn't – and Uncle Ted, who was not very practical, thought he'd seen one somewhere, but couldn't remember quite where. Aunty Alice said that he wouldn't know what a blowlamp looked like even if he were to fall over it, so in the end Mum and Aunt Alice bought one from the hardware shop on Abbeydale Road, and shared the cost.

So, now we had the tools, we could begin the job. All the existing paint in the living room was to be burnt off, and I had the dubious honour of assisting in this task. It seemed to go on for ever. Three doors, a double floor-to-ceiling cupboard – all panelled – and the window frame and skirting board. It was murder on the hands. As the bubbling paint was scraped away, it had a tendency to fall in splotches onto the hand holding the scraper, which caused me to have blisters and burn marks for weeks. There were, of course, lighter moments, and we often repaired outside, into the sunshine, to sit on the garden steps for a cup of tea.

One day the news arrived, by the very efficient neighbourhood bush telegraph, that the very first delivery since the War began, of Wall's ice cream, had arrived at the sweet shop at the bottom of Woodseats Road. I quickly downed tools, sped over the bridge, and joined the not inconsiderable queue. (In those days, if one was passing a shop and there was a queue outside, it was policy to join on to the end. Even if one didn't know what was being sold, it was a fair bet that it would be something in very short supply.) I can still remember the taste of that delicious ice cream, and the way we sat, me perched on the top of the step-ladder, and Mum and Aunty Alice on the chairs, still covered in old sheeting, in the midst of all the debris of decorating, savouring every mouthful.

After the burning off, the woodwork had to be rubbed down well, and then the artistic bit began. As the new paint was being applied, a comb had to be gently scraped along behind the brush, thus forming a pattern as the original wood began to show through. I was beginning to enjoy the spring cleaning when we got to this part of the procedure, and we had some wonderful patterns on our woodwork in the living room for years afterwards. Distemper and colour wash was still the only thing obtainable for the walls, but the choice of colours was improving. That particular Spring, as I recall, we used buttercup yellow, and the finished effect was quite effective. War or not, Mum always did the best she could to make the house as pleasant as possible, and we were never ashamed to take anyone home, because it always looked like a palace to us.

By this time, Brenda had been working for a few months, and was taking shorthand and typing lessons, two evenings a week, at Abbeydale School. Each Friday, after the lessons, there was a social evening, which we could both attend. We were very fond of dancing, and it was at one of these events that we had the idea of going to a dancing school to learn a bit of Latin American. We knew the basics of all the usual dances, but each time a Tango or a Rumba was announced, we had to sit it out, not knowing the first thing about either of them. I didn't have very much money to pay for such lessons, but we were always very expert at working things out between us, and with my meagre pocket money and her wages, we managed to enrol in a class on Abbeydale Road.

We had only one lesson, as it turned out, which happened to be the Empress Tango. I don't believe that any two people ever had as much fun as we did that evening. There were so many people in that room, and almost all of them seemed to have aspirations to become the second Fred Astaire or Ginger Rodgers. Brenda and I were convulsed with laughter, as little fat men and large ladies swept around the room, tripping the light fantastic, whilst the instructor gave us directions and instructions from the centre of the floor. There were many collisions, mostly caused by Brenda and I, but we finally got the hang of it, and considered our shilling each as money well spent. Looking back, we must have been a pain in the elbow when we were young, but we had some good times. We were both inveterate gigglers, and could see the funny side of every situation. At home, it was the same. The three of us could collapse with laughing, usually at the dining table, where it was viewed as a mortal sin to even talk when at the table.

Another of Mum's favourite adages was, 'Let your meat stop your mouth', but as all gigglers know, once started it is very difficult to stop. Usually Dad would give us one of his stern looks, but that only made things worse, and I have seen times in my life when even Mum and Dad would join in. Giggling can be very infectious.

We had a black bakelite radio at home, which took pride of place on a shelf above Dad's chair. All through the War we would listen to all the programmes designed to lift the spirits of the populace. Gathered round the fire on cold winter nights, (coal had to be used sparingly too, and to save fuel, Mum had placed a fire brick in the grate, which was only removed when the oven was in use, to allow the heat to be drawn under the oven bottom), we were entertained by many great artists of the period. Our favourites as children were the comedians, Tommy Handley in *ITMA* and Robb Wilton with his side-splitting accounts that began 'The day War broke out, my missus said to me . . .', Albert Modley and Gert and Daisy, and Mrs Feather's rambling conversations over the telephone to Mr Bullock the butcher. Each morning and afternoon there would be *Music while you Work*, with its very distinctive signature tune, and each lunchtime a short variety show, usually broadcast from a factory canteen 'somewhere in England' during the worker's lunchbreak. I first heard Stefan Grappelli during these broadcasts, and Stainless Stephen, who was a Sheffield man. There was no television in those times, but the radio more than made up for that. The BBC put out some wonderful programmes during the war years, and deserve great credit for it.

By April 1945, it was plain that the War was almost ended. As the Russians entered Berlin, the news came that Adolph Hitler and his new wife, Eva Braun, had committed suicide in their bunker, but many Nazis escaped to other parts of the world, including Martin Borman, who became one of the most sought-after Nazis in post-war years, though he was never found. Mum never believed that he was dead, but then again she thought the same thing about Hitler, and was always expecting him to pop up somewhere, waving his swastikas around and restarting all the mayhem once again. On May 7th, General Jodl signed the document of unconditional surrender, and the War in Europe was finally over.

In Britain, a national holiday was proclaimed, and Victory in Europe Day – better known as VE Day – was celebrated in every city, town, village and hamlet in the country. Street parties were the order of the day, and flags and bunting were in abundance everywhere. In Sheffield, we had our very own decorated tram, which plied its way on every route in the city, draped in red, white and blue bunting and massive V for Victory signs and fairy lights which could be seen for miles, glowing from every possible space.

In the evening, Brenda and I joined the hundreds of people walking to the City centre, to celebrate in Barker's Pool, and for once we threw caution to the winds. With most of the young people from the Youth Club we walked, arm in arm, six or seven abreast, along Abbeydale Roads towards town, singing and laughing and generally enjoying the moment. We walked all the way into Barker's Pool and were met with a sight of utter jubilation. The whole of Sheffield seemed to be there on that night, laughing, singing and dancing around. Civilians, members of the armed forces, young people, old people, children. They were waving flags, kissing and embracing everyone within reach, so we all merrily joined in.We didn't care that evening whether we were seen with the lads or not, it was a night to savour, never to be repeated in our lifetime, and we determined to enjoy it to the full.

During the last week in May, I received the long-awaited letter from the General Post Office, and on June 2nd my working life commenced. I well remember alighting from the tram in Fitzalan Square on that first morning, well-scrubbed and complete with sandwiches and all the paraphernalia necessary for one's first excursion into the adult world of the working girl. I was full of hope at the prospect of becoming, eventually, a GPO-trained telephonist, and as I entered the building I was almost walking on air. Looking back, after almost a lifetime of switchboard operating, I can only think that I must have been a very strange girl and should probably have been certified on the spot. My letter was handed over at the door and I was directed to a small room in the basement to await the arrival of the supervisor. There was another girl waiting there, a girl with whom I was to become great friends over the following years. Her name was Brenda, too, and to avoid confusion, I always referred to her in conversation as work-Brenda. We awaited the arrival of the supervisor with some trepidation, as we surveyed our gloomy surroundings.

I had the advantage over my companion when it came to supervisors, because I had already been told by Margaret what to expect. As we were to discover in the weeks that followed, GPO supervisors, in the main, were very formidable ladies, and their orders and instructions were never to be taken lightly. Most of them had probably been employed there from the day that Alexander Graham Bell had invented the telephone, and their outlook on life, and their attitude toward the younger people in their charge would not have been out of place in a Victorian workhouse.

The lady who came in to greet us was a prime example. She was a tall, very angular person of indeterminate age, sporting a headphone hairstyle, with plaits worn coiled around her ears, extremely handy in her line of work, I remember thinking. It was not so much a greeting which we received, there was no, 'Good morning, girls, welcome to the GPO', or anything of that kind, it was more a very long list of what would, or would not, be expected from the pair of us if we were to continue in the employ of the Post Office for the foreseeable future.

The list of 'dont's' was endless. The main ones seemed to be formulated specifically to make a young girl's life as miserable as possible. She placed great emphasis on the subject of non-fraternisation between probationers and their male counterparts, the messenger boys. These were the callow youths who spent their working days either pedalling frantically around the city on their sit-up-and-beg bicycles delivering telegrams, or in the Telegram Room, which was located on the ground floor corridor. This particular room, the lady informed us, was to be avoided at all times. Apparently, these youths spent much of their time whilst in the building, hanging around the Telegram Room door, waiting to pounce on any unsuspecting probationer who happened to be passing by. We would not, repeat not, she stated, speak to these boys under any circumstances, and any infraction of this rule would be looked upon as a very serious matter, and could result in dismissal. I can remember reflecting gloomily, that, between Post Office rulings and my mother, I should be very fortunate indeed ever to get myself a husband, and would most probably spend my whole life in the employ of the GPO, and finish up lecturing young people in the manner of this Hitler-in-knickers who was lecturing us.

As the weeks went by, of course, we quickly realised that things were not half so bad as we had been led to suppose in that first interview. A lot of the things we were told were merely a reflection of the interviewer's own views on life, and perhaps unfortunately, the said messengers didn't seem to have a pounce between them. Actually, we had many organised socials in the canteen on Saturday evenings between Messengers and Probationers, and these occasions soon became one of the highlights of our working lives.

The office to which we were eventually taken on that first morning, was not the Telephone Exchange, as we had expected, but the Instrument Room. This was where the teleprinters were located. It was quite a large room, flanked on two sides by large windows, which looked out on one side to the Park district of Sheffield, and Flat Street on the other. The teleprinters were positioned along both sides of three large tables, down the middle of which were moving belts. As the operators received the messages, they would tear them from the strips of teleprinter tape and stick them onto telegram forms. These were then placed on the belt, where they moved along to drop into the hoppers at the end of the tables. One of our tasks was to collect these, sort them into destinations, and either take them to the switchboard operators at the far end of the room to be telephoned through, or pop them into the suction tube, in their yellow envelopes, to be sucked straight through to the Telegram Room for delivery. A lot of unauthorised messages found their way down that tube over the years, as I remember.

Our duties were quite varied, and not particularly taxing, and until we reached the age of seventeen we were more or less the general dogsbodies in most of the Post Office departments. We were issued with the most hideous bottle-green overalls on our first day, and they were to be our uniform for the following three years. All probationers worked a six-day week, and our duties were covered by a six-week rota. Within any six week period, Saturdays included, we could be on duty from 8.00 am until 4.00 pm one week, 8.30 am until 4.30 pm the next, and so on until we reached 12.00 noon to 8.00 pm, after which we would revert back to the 8.00 am start, and begin the cycle all over again. Added to all this, we worked a four-hour Sunday duty every four or five weeks, for which we were paid overtime, and, if scheduled, any Bank Holiday including Christmas Day and Boxing Day. My starting wage was the princely sum of 12/6d per week, or in today's coinage 62 pence. Out of this I was allowed to keep half-a-crown (12$\frac{1}{2}$ pence) for myself and Mum had the rest, although she provided my fares to and from work on the tram.

Hilda was to join us at the GPO the following year, and from then on we were always referred to collectively as 'The Axelby girls'. It was only a few weeks ago that I bumped into one of the girls who worked with us in those far off days. We were in the lift at Telephone House, and as we reached the ground floor she said. 'Aren't you one of the

Axelby girls?' I replied that I was and she asked, 'Which one were you?'
I replied – as I always do when asked the same question – 'I was the
quiet one.' Not strictly true, but when compared with Hilda, who was
always the life and soul of any party and who could even make the
Supervisors laugh, I was a virtual mouse. Despite having three telephone operator daughters, it took us years to persuade Mum to have a
telephone installed. Her excuse? 'I can't be doing with those new fan-
gled inventions in my house!'

During my time as a Probationer, I was fortunate enough to work in
quite a few different departments, including Wireless Records, where
we were responsible for sending out license reminders for anyone own-
ing a radio, (televisions were unheard of in those days). I also worked
at the counter from where the telegrams were sent in the main Post
Office, and this was one of my favourite places, although we were only
sent down to help at extra busy times and were only allowed to stick
the stamps onto the forms as they were handed to the counter clerks.
I was eventually sent to work at Telephone Buildings at the bottom of
West Street, which was the best of all – a nine-to-five job with half-day
Saturdays and no Bank Holiday duties – sheer bliss.

In spite of everything, I always look back on those days as a very
happy time. I made lots of friends and have many happy memories of
time spent with them. Humour was essential and we had plenty of
that. We never took things very seriously; after all, we were young and
full of life, and every new day was an adventure. We were growing up
and there were things to do, and places to go and people to meet. There
was going to be a new world out there, and we were to be a part of it.
It was a time for hope, for putting the bad years firmly behind us, and
for looking to the future. With childhood behind us and family respon-
sibilities years ahead, this was a time for fun, and we made the most of
every minute.

The ending of the war in the Pacific came surprisingly swiftly, in
August 1945, after two atomic bombs had been dropped on Japan. Most
laymen had expected hostilities to last at least another year, or even
more. We were under no illusion regarding the tenacity of the Japanese,
who were expected to fight to the last man, woman and child. Fire

raids on Japanese towns were regularly taking place.

Since the War, many efforts have been made to understand the complicated mentality of the Japanese. Their head of state, Emperor Hirohito, was no carpet-chewing megalomaniac – he was a god, and his subjects worshipped him as such. The armed services and civilian population considered surrender as the greatest dishonour, and treated their captives accordingly. When the survivors of Japanese prisoner-of-war camps emerged from captivity in 1945, the western world was horrified at the barbaric treatment they had received. And the arguments put forward over the years in philosophic mitigation for the treatment of these men, has never made a scrap of difference to me.

I can remember vividly seeing the newsreel pictures of pitiful, half-starved men, barely able to stand, being helped to walk or being stretchered on board the ships which took them to hospitals and rehabilitation centres in India and elsewhere. For most of these men it was to be months before they were fit enough to return home to their families, and the lives from which they had been uprooted at the beginning of hostilities. Cinema audiences were reduced to tears by the pictures, but I think the underlying mood was of great anger, an anger which has never left me after all these many years.

I have never pretended to be an expert on the subject of warfare, and consider myself just an ordinary person, now a grandmother, and I readily accept that a nuclear war has been avoided by these deterrents. But conventional wars have been taking place almost every year since I can remember on this planet of ours, and people are still being killed and discriminated against because of the colour of their skin, or because of the religion which they practice, or for some other, equally obscure reason. Mankind doesn't seem to have learned much over the centuries, and if I could have but one wish before I shake the proverbial seven, it would be for greed and prejudice to disappear overnight and for everyone to live in harmony with his neighbour.

Grandma Wilson once said to me when I was a little girl, 'Nothing will ever change in this world of ours, until the system is altered. I will never live to see it, but I hope that you will.' Well, I am still waiting for things to change, and I shall probably be saying the same sort of thing to my grand-daughter when she is old enough to understand. I hope that some day she may read this meander through my past and draw her own conclusions. Perhaps she will, with the confidence of youth, dismiss it all as the ramblings of a silly old biddy, well past her sell-by date, but I hope not. In any event, it may be of some assistance to her when she takes her history lessons at school.

Her mother – my daughter – used to think that when I was a little girl, dinosaurs still roamed at will over the earth, but if Rebecca ever reads this, at least she will know that the only dinosaurs around during my childhood were the tanks, planes and warships and all the millions of men, armed to the teeth, waiting for the opportunity to knock seven bells out of each other, in the old time-honoured fashion.

War regulations restrict Bulmer's Cider to certain areas. Soon we hope Bulmer's will once again be greeting old friends and making new ones everywhere

Bulmer's
CIDER

H. P. BULMER & CO., LTD., HEREFORD   royds 76d

If you have enjoyed this book . . .

SHEAF **P**UBLISHING produces a wide range of well-known books about Sheffield and its surrounding area. Our photographic collections from Peter Harvey and Stephen McClarence, and Valerie Salim's two books on Sheffield Ghosts are particularly well-known, but these are just a small part of our lists.

You can find our books in all good local bookshops, but in case of difficulty just write to us at 35 Mooroaks Road, Sheffield 10 or telephone 273 9067 for a complete up-to-date list of all our books in print.

Buying our books couldn't be easier! If you can't get to the shops easily, just phone us and we will arrange delivery direct to your home. And for that special present, we will even post books to your friends.

And if *you* think you have a book inside you that no-one else has written yet, let us know, preferably before you start writing. We're always ready to look at ideas for new books about Sheffield!